LIFE IS BEST
SERVED SOBER

GRANT ROLLEY

Published by Obol House Publishing Company
An imprint of Huntsville Independent Press

103 Spenryn Drive, Madison, AL 35758

Life Is Best Served Sober is a work of creative nonfiction based on the author's personal experiences and reflections. While every effort has been made to present events accurately, some names, details, and circumstances may have been changed to respect privacy and narrative flow. The opinions expressed are those of the author and do not necessarily reflect the views of the publisher.

Obol House can bring authors to your live event. For more information or to book an event, contact Obol House Publishing Company at +1 (256) 678-0411 or visit our website at: www. ObolHouse.com

Cover design by HMDPUBLISHING

Interior design by HMDPUBLISHING

The text for this book was set in Proxima Nova.

Manufactured in the United States of America
First Obol House paperback edition December 2024
1 2 3 4 5 6 7 8 9 10

The Library of Congress has cataloged this edition as follows:
Names: Rolley, Grant, author.
Title: *Life Is Best Served Sober*

Identifiers: ISBN: 979-8-9905049-5-0 (pbk)
ISBN: 979-8-9905049-6-7 (hc)
ISBN: 979-8-9905049-7-4 (eBook)

CONTENTS

CHAPTER 1:

STARTING LINE

Marshall said he would leave my name at the security gate. I was looking forward to this job interview, and the opportunity to be the tennis instructor at a resort in Tampa, Florida. Most of my instruction so far had been with parks and recreation, at private golf and racket clubs, as well as one-on-one personal instruction. A resort atmosphere like Paradise Lakes Resort would allow me a constant turnover of new tennis players and students of varying abilities. The resort atmosphere also tends to attract people willing to spend a lot of money on fun.

It was 1986, and I was 24 years old. Getting a job was my top priority, as I had just moved to Tampa from Ft. Lauderdale, and I had a part-time afternoon gig with Joe Brandi, the tournament director and tennis professional at the St. Petersburg Tennis Center. Joe is a well-respected tennis instructor who worked with several successful tennis professionals. He would eventually coach Pete Sampras to win his first grand slam at the 1990 U.S. Open a few years later.

My not yet having a job prevented me from being able to pay him for lessons, but he had seen me play recently and thought highly enough of my skills to give me lessons in exchange for my helping him work with some junior players at his club. I had recently dropped out of the

University of Wisconsin-Oshkosh and was in recovery at the time from drugs and alcohol. I was several months clean and sober, and all the better for it.

In fact, that's how I came to get the coaching interview at Paradise Lakes. After sharing with my Alcoholics Anonymous group that I needed a job as soon as possible, a guy came up to me after the meeting and handed me Marshall's business card.

"I know they recently lost their tennis pro, and there's an opening. Give Marshall a call." he said.

The resort was located a little north of Tampa in a city called Lutz in Pascoe County, about a 45-minute drive up Interstate 275 from St. Pete. As I made the drive, I had time to reflect on the past couple of years of my life.

Following my first 28-day stint at the Pinewood Drug and Alcohol Rehab in Ft. Lauderdale, I was alcohol-free for 100 days. Like most people who have not accepted the reality of being an alcoholic, I mistakenly assumed I no longer had a drinking problem. I had not yet been to an Alcoholics Anonymous meeting or met my AA sponsor, Charles Edson, so I still didn't realize I was an alcoholic, with very little psychological control over my addiction, at that point.

Not acknowledging that my DUI in Wisconsin the previous summer, which led to my stint at Pinewood, was any more than just a bad mistake, I decided it was time to move on from it.

I reasoned that I could drink the night before my days off work. That would be my set-aside days for lying out by the swimming pool and drinking. After a couple of weeks, I decided I could go out a little bit on Saturday night because I only worked half a day Sunday and didn't have to go in until after lunch.

Like anything that does not have limitations and guardrails, an alcoholic cannot stop pushing the envelope looking for the next level high. There must always be something better out there, and we crave it like nobody's business.

I had a great job teaching tennis at Bonaventure Racket Club in Weston, just thirty minutes from Ft. Lauderdale. But things took a turn when I started buying cocaine from a neighbor in my apartment complex. Life began spiraling out of control faster than I could keep up. In hindsight, it was really the cocaine that landed me in rehab for the second time, even more-so than the alcohol. A few months had passed since then, and after fully committing myself to AA, I quit my job at Bonaventure and moved to Florida's west coast to start fresh, embracing a life of sobriety and freedom from drugs.

Marshall's instructions said turn left off North Dale Mabry Boulevard onto Brinson Road. Brinson was heavily wooded on both sides, but I was driving parallel to Mabry for about a mile or so. I noticed that this place was obviously tucked well back off the main road, not thinking anything of it in the moment.

A little ways up, I turned left again onto Paradise Lakes Boulevard, and I continued to drive deeper into what was obviously a quiet and secluded little village. When I reached the intersection of Paradise Lakes and Vista del Sol Circle, I realized there were, in-fact, several secluded vacation spots hidden from view by the main road. Eventually, I came to a small lake with a sign that said Paradise Lake. The road ended at a gate on the right, leading into a community of villas that lined the left side.

I gave my name at the gate and the guard waved me through. I could see the pool and tennis courts up ahead on the right, but I got distracted by what looked like two completely naked women walking along the road in front of the villas talking. I only got a glimpse before they turned into a corridor going into the villas.

I figured they must have been wearing nude-colored bathing clothes or something. I was trying to focus on where I was going, and only saw them for a moment. My eyes must have been playing tricks. Maybe they thought no one would notice this far off the beaten path, but I'm not sure how - after all, they were casually strolling down the main road into the resort! I shrugged it off as no big deal; women go topless at beaches in South Florida all the time.

I saw the tennis courts and pulled into a parking space in front of them. It was a large and sprawling layout, well landscaped with tropical flora and varying species of palm trees and bromeliads, just like all Florida resorts in those days. I got out of my car and walked along the sidewalk to the pool where there was a smoking grill with several whole chickens rotating deliciously on a rotisserie.

There was also a poolside snack bar. I didn't see anyone at first but as I reached the counter, a woman poked her head up from behind the counter. "Can I help you?" she asked casually as she stood up, her full bare breasts and midriff exposed from behind the bar.

"Y-yes," I stammered. "I have an appointment with Marshall."

"Two doors down on the left," she pointed.

Okaaay then, I mused. I walked down a short corridor and opened the door. A buck-naked woman, who I assumed was Marshall's receptionist, stood up from her desk and asked again, somewhat provocatively this time, "How can I help you?"

I know it is hard to believe, but I still did not catch on to why no one had on any clothes. You'd understand if you knew me then. Maybe I was in one of those repetitive dream sequences where everyone, but you remembered to put on clothes that morning, only this one was in reverse, and I was the only one clothed.

"I'm here to see Marshall," I said, suddenly terrified I may be about to see more of Marshall than I wanted!

She yelled, "Marshall!"

To my relief, Marshall walked out bare-chested, but wearing a pair of shorts.

"Hey old buddy," he said putting out his hand to shake. "Apparently we have a mutual friend in AA."

We exchanged niceties and then he came right out with the offer.

"If you want the tennis instructor's job, it's yours," he said. "No salary. You are an independent contractor so you can charge whatever you like for lessons and keep all the money. We don't take a commission. You can set your own hours and clothing is optional."

"I see," I said. "Are there any other tennis instructors on the property?"

"No, we had one, but he disappeared," Marshall said. "You're it if you take the job."

"Did he take his clothes with him when he left," I asked.

"We don't know. He just never showed back up."

I learned through sobriety to count every blessing. I needed a job, and now I had one, so I accepted.

My name is Grant Rolley, and I am a recovered alcoholic, 40 years sober. I have spent the last 38 years as the tennis teaching professional at Musgrove Country Club in Jasper, Alabama; and I have been either officially or unofficially coaching tennis at Jasper High School (formerly Walker High School) for almost as long.

I'm what people call a transplanted southerner. I was born in Milwaukee, Wisconsin and grew up in Minocqua, Wisconsin, but I spent a great deal of my first seven years of life in Lutcher, Louisiana. After dropping out of UW-Oshkosh, I spent most of my young adult life in Ft. Lauderdale and Tampa.

I have been playing tennis since I was a little boy at summer camp and teaching or coaching tennis since I was in high school. I have never been a professional athlete, but I have always been a darn good one. I also played basketball, football, softball, and even ran cross country; But there's something about playing with balls that I always missed! You may notice I am a bit of a jokester, and I tend to attract some real characters as well, as you will see.

One of my all-time favorite athletes is Brett Favre. I first saw him play in a game that has stayed with me for years— when Southern Mississippi beat Alabama at Legion Field in Birmingham. Brett brought such joy and excitement to the game, and he kept doing so for decades in the NFL. His toughness was unparalleled; he never missed a game in 20 years, no matter what challenges came his way.

Now, Brett faces an even greater challenge: living with Parkinson's disease. Despite that, I still admire him deeply, not just for his resilience on the field but for the strength he continues to show in life. Even as he faces Parkinson's, my wish remains for him to live a long and fulfilling life. He is often in my prayers, a reminder of the impact he has had on so many.

I have maintained amateur status my entire career, winning 57 tennis tournaments including singles, doubles and mixed doubles spanning a period consisting of junior high school, high school, college men's, open men's 25, 30, 35, 40 and 45 age divisions. My students have won 13 state high school championships, and I have seen over 30 players earn college tennis scholarships, including several kids I coached in Minocqua and Tampa.

In 2018, I was honored to be inducted into the Alabama Tennis Hall of Fame. Earlier in my career, in 1982, I was ranked No. 32 in singles and, in 1986, No. 18 in men's open doubles by the USPTA (United States Professional Tennis Association), alongside my friend Ross Dubins from Miami Beach. Ross is not only an incredible tennis player but also a great friend. He and his wife, Veronica, are wonderful people, and their two daughters both went on to play Division I tennis at the University of Miami and the University of Central Florida.

The USPTA represents tennis professionals across all 50 states, and achieving that doubles ranking with Ross remains one of my proudest accomplishments.

After my Hall of Fame induction, my lifetime goal became winning a Gold Ball—the equivalent of a National Championship in your age division in tennis. I was also featured in 78 Magazine in Jasper: The Madman of Minocqua.

These experiences have sparked my interest in motivational speaking. So, if you're interested, I encourage you to look up 'Grant Rolley Tennis' and watch my Hall of Fame speech. People have said it was good—but I'll let you be the judge.

People say I could have made a lot of money teaching semi-pro, and perhaps I could have played the professional circuit, but in the early days when I was young, I spent too much time drinking, smoking and doing drugs. Fortunately, I got a grip on it by my early twenties, and since then I have remained in what I call the minor leagues of tennis.

My good friend Charlie Owens, who is Alabama's best professional tennis pro and, in my opinion, the best overall athlete I have ever met, finished his professional career ranked No. 35 in the world in singles. I asked him once why he never ranked higher on the professional circuit, and his answer sounded familiar.

"I liked to party too much, Grant," he said. "I stayed up until 4:30 in the mornings drinking and singing in rock and country music bands. When I wasn't doing that, I was turkey hunting."

That conversation reminded me of one of my favorite musicians, Jerry Jeff Walker - a man who knew how to blend a wild spirit with soulful music. If Charlie had ever taken a stage with Jerry Jeff, I'm sure they'd have had the crowd on their feet until sunrise.

Personally, I can't sing, and I know a lot of turkeys but don't hunt them. However, I did enough drinking until the wee hours of the morning to cover for myself and make up for what Charlie missed.

Despite everything, I've lived what I consider a happy and successful life, especially when you think about the reckless path I was on in high school and college. My greatest achievement, however - my match point, if you will - was defeating alcohol and drugs. For me, the drugs were always secondary to the alcohol. Alcoholism is a rollercoaster for most people - a life spent in and out of rehabilitation facilities, "drying out," all so they can start over again and drink in moderation going forward.

That is what we tell ourselves, 'I have it under control *this time*.' But the sad reality is that when alcoholics drink, they can't stop. It isn't a matter of wanting to stop, knowing they need to stop, or someone trying to make them stop. People who suffer from Alcohol Use Disorder (AUD) cannot stop without help. Even then, it is usually a lifelong fight not to turn back to alcohol, especially when facing life's challenges, trials and tribulations.

That is the difference between people who drink - even people who drink a lot - and those who are alcoholics like me. That being said, I don't condemn drinking. I have learned there are many types of drinkers — teens and college kids who mostly binge drink; problem drinkers who partake in times of crisis; weekend drinkers who party-hearty as a break from a hard week of working, but who go back to work on Monday fully sober and lucid; social drinkers who only drink with friends and at events and on special occasions; and don't forget the casual drinkers, who only drink occasionally or in small amounts.

The problem arises when one out of every ten drinkers discover they cannot stop drinking. Once they start, they cannot slow down or moderate themselves. Those people are true alcoholics.

For sure, those years of drinking were not something to be proud of in my life, so why look back at the past to relive it now, so many years later? The answer is three years ago after fully recovering from a stroke that threatened my life in 2020, I was giving a tennis lesson to a lady in her late 70s. She had recently been diagnosed with cancer but refused to stop playing tennis.

"Grant," she asked me, "I'm sure there is a long list of crazy things you did when drinking, but what is the craziest thing that happened to you sober?"

"I coached a nudist colony tennis team to a big statewide tennis tournament win in Florida," I told her.

She chuckled. "The good Lord is not done with you yet, Grant. You could have died recently with that stroke, and probably many times before during your drinking days, but you didn't.

"Write a book and share your story. It will be good for you and a blessing to others."

So, I took her advice. If in some small way my story gives hope to other alcoholics who doubt their own strength and resolve, well, all it will take is compelling one problem drinker to get clean and sober, and it will have been worth it.

If you are not an alcoholic but an athlete who just enjoys reading about the crazy antics of a 65-year-old tennis instructor with a bunch of colorful characters as friends, then maybe you will get a laugh or two.

It is sometimes painful and even embarrassing to relive, but while not a rip-roaring adventure or sexy tale of romance, I hope it touches someone who needs to hear it, because I need to tell it.

There were two aspects of my early life that are characterized by most mental health professionals as destabilizing factors in any adult person's life. One was the lack of a father in the home; the second was constant relocation. The second is often the result of the first.

These two factors alone make individuals in similar circumstances prime candidates for alcoholism as adults. Research conducted by the American Psychological Association in their Journal of Personality and Social Psychology shows that school performance, problematic behavior, and low self-esteem as adults are prevalent in children who were frequently uprooted from home, school, and stable relationships.

I was subjected to a new school and new friends many times during my childhood and adolescence, so I definitely match the profile. But just to be clear, I was a terrible student and despised school—not because I didn't have a father in my home, though that caused anxiety and abandonment issues separate from academics. My struggles in school stemmed from what I now know to be attention deficit disorder and hyperactivity disorder.

It wasn't that I lacked intelligence or had a learning disability. It was because I was a natural athlete, who needed to be moving - anticipating and responding to what was going on around me - rather than sitting in a chair for hours and hours, listening to the droning of a lecture about atoms, molecules, or solving geometry equations into infinity.

I will admit though that after I started drinking at age 14, some behavioral issues certainly arose from it. For example, one night after drinking three glasses of Kool-Aid spiked with ground mushrooms, I went outside in a blizzard and ripped the windshield wiper blades off my car. While dozens of my friends hung outside the window laughing, I pretended to be "protecting everyone from the snow" by brushing the blades back and forth across my face.

Of course, there was also that time my friend Lenny and I dropped acid and pilfered a sofa from a student's front porch, then carried it down the middle of the street claiming we were "moving" to Madison, Wisconsin... two hours away.

Oh, and I nearly forgot that time my friend Barry Lesieur and I skipped out on paying for breakfast at Shoney's and I spent 10 days in the local lock-up.

Okay, okay, I guess those unfortunate examples prove the point of the research study, but I have never suffered from low self-esteem! I liked being the class clown. I enjoyed the attention. I was proud of it. In terms of myself and my sister both being recovered alcoholics, there are two other risk factors that left the two of us vulnerable to AUD. AA and the Alcohol Rehab Guide name biologic and environmental conditions as leading risk factors as well.

There are over 50 genes that scientists believe are related to drinking problems and those genes are known to be passed down through generations within families with the genes. Chemicals in those genes are triggered when a person experiences the pleasure related to drinking alcohol, and that strong impulse to repeat the behavior becomes almost obsessive.

You have heard the phrase, "I can't get enough." That is me on alcohol. My problem was not drinking, but the inability to stop drinking once I started. The experts also list environmental factors like proximity to liquor stores and access to alcohol as contributing risks and I cannot deny any of that either.

In Minocqua, where we moved when I was in 8th grade, there were 100 taverns within 15 miles of each other starting with the Yacht Club on one end of the bridge, and the Thirsty Whale on the other end. Drinking is a pastime in Wisconsin and in Minocqua, it started young.

One of my closest friends, Richard Simmons, his parents owned a tavern called Bethel's Bar in Minocqua, literally blocks down the street from the high school. Bethels sponsored all our intramural basketball, softball and tennis teams and was not only the place to celebrate after wins, but they gave us unlimited access to beer before and after events and road trips. Most of the boys I hung out with when I was underage were of legal age.

While as an adult I do not doubt those effects on my life overall, comparatively speaking, I still believe I adjusted well to constant relocation because of my personality. I used my spontaneous wit and innate sense of humor to light up a room and make people laugh. That made it easy for me to make friends. I also had a constant in my life. That was athletics. From Pee Wee football to basketball, softball, and later tennis, wherever we moved, I made myself part of a team.

But that is not to say the lack of a father didn't have its effects. Absolutely, it did, especially when I was young. My mom didn't intentionally set out to frustrate me when it came to my father, but it ended up that way anyhow. The hardship and pain she endured when my father left her made it difficult for her to explain to a little kid. In that void, a lot of resentment grew.

CHAPTER 2:

NO LOVE LOST

I was a year old, and my sister Robin was almost three when my dad, Wayne Rolley left us and my 21-year-old mom Sarah. Mom became a single mother of two with $8 to her name over the course of a single night.

Overwhelmed and broke, she went to work for her parents, Richard - who I always called Dick - and Helen Wittenkamp. Dick was a district forest ranger for the Wisconsin Conservation Department. In 1937, he purchased land on Clear Lake in Wisconsin's Northwoods from two brothers on which stood an old sawmill, along with a fishing and hunting camp in Woodruff, Wisconsin.

There, "Mr. and Mrs. Dubs", as the campers called them, established the Red Pine Camp for Girls, which is still one of Wisconsin's longest running summer camps.

Working through the summers as a camp director, my mom befriended another camp instructor named Irene Boudreaux. Irene and her husband had no children, but they did have a home in Lutcher, Louisiana that she returned to every fall.

About the time my mom and dad split, Irene's husband died suddenly in an electrical accident. Both she and Mom, having recently experienced devastating losses, ReRe, as Robin and I called her, invited the three of us to come live with her in their now big, empty house in Lutcher. Many years later, in 1972 when my grandparents, both of whom lived well into their 90s, retired, my mom and ReRe took over the camp as its directors. For ReRe's loyalty to the camp and to his family, Dick built her a house at Red Pine Camp.

Overall, it was a wonderful experience for us and a blessing to my mom at that time. For seven years, we traveled every summer to Red Pine Camp for Mom and ReRe to work, and then returned to Lutcher in the fall in time for school to start.

Located in St. James Parish on the east bank of the Mississippi River, Lutcher lies between Baton Rouge and New Orleans but is considered part of the New Orleans metropolitan area.

During the school year, ReRe coached basketball at Lutcher High School, so she walked Robin and I to the school bus every morning on her way to work. She came from a large family with seven brothers, and she is the one who first took me to gyms for exercise and practice. She taught me how to use the backboard to make bank shots in basketball.

I never had a basketball lesson, but I credit ReRe with teaching me the basics. As I got older, I added speed, strength and agility, resulting in my becoming a first-rate point guard at Lakeland Union High School. ReRe followed up summer camp training by putting up a basketball goal in the backyard at our house in Lutcher, and she taught me and my best friend, a little black kid named Craig Williams, how to dribble and shoot.

We lived on 2nd Street, next door to a large Cajun family named the Duhes. They had nine children - eight boys and one girl. There were so many Duhes kids that it was a neighborhood joke that they had enough children to form their own football team and play against themselves.

There was a wide-open empty lot one street over on 3ʳᵈ Street and that is where the Duhes and neighborhood kids played pickup football, basketball, and softball.

Dreaming of one day playing for the LSU Tigers, football was our favorite game. There was significant size differentiation due to the varying ages of the kids, so we had our own version of the game. Craig and I often joined in.

I remember when Hurricane Betsy struck the Gulf Coast in 1965, it brought widespread damage to coastal Florida, Mississippi and Louisiana. There were torn and jagged roof shingles strewn all over the neighborhood and in the streets.

I was just a little kid, and one day one of the Duhes kids and I got into a shingles fight, sailing them through the air at each other like deadly saw-edged frisbees. Guess who lost the battle? Yep, along with my two front teeth. I still remember it being very painful and leaving me with caps on my front teeth to this day.

It was also in Lutcher, spending time with the Duhes, that I first noticed something - or rather someone - was missing from our home. Every afternoon just after five o'clock, a man they called 'Daddy' arrived home from work. Mr. Duhes would go in and change clothes, then come back out shortly before dinner and join in the football games. We scored a lot more touchdowns with Mr. Duhes as our quarterback.

I noticed he did other things too, like bandaging knees when we hit the ground a little too hard, grilling steak and fish on the outdoor barbecue pit, and taking his kids to crawfish boils and Mardi Gras parades. He was always home at night to help them with their homework, and always there in the morning to take them to school.

I seemed to be missing this 'daddy'. Why? "Do I have a Daddy?" I repeatedly asked Mom. "You have your grandfather who is a very nice man," Mom would reply.

What a cryptic answer for a young boy! At the time, I had to let it go at that, but such a murky answer would not withstand the passage of time or the growing curiosity of a young boy. As I grew older, I had a lot of questions haunting me about this daddy and I wanted answers.

If I had a dad, why did he leave? Why does no one want to talk about him? Where is he? Does my father know about me? What is he like? Why has he not tried to contact me? Is he as curious about me as I am about him? Does he know where to find me?

I know now I was too young to understand, but my mother's sense of peace and easy distraction from the hard questions wouldn't last forever.

Mom was right about my grandfather, though. Some of my fondest memories from childhood are of Dick and my grandmother, who all of the campers called "The Duchess."

Dick was naturally very outdoorsy. He taught me how to reel in my first cold water trout and how to build a campfire; he taught me the difference between poison oak and ivy and other woodsy plants. He and his camps were crucial to my early childhood development. He gave me a safe space to grow and learn and ask questions, and more importantly, provided us with all the love and comfort of home - which included introducing me to what would always be my saving grace - sports.

I was too young to go to Towering Pines Boys Camp, 25 miles away, so Dick let me hang out at Red Pines with Mom and ReRe until I was old enough to become nothing but a nuisance to the girls. Red Pine Camp had everything - basketball, football, boating, swimming, waterskiing, tennis, and fishing to name a few. The first sport ReRe introduced me to at camp was basketball, but it's also where I first played tennis. They had three tennis courts, and I learned to swing by volleying a ball against a practice wall.

Sports helped distract me from the more difficult aspects of childhood and adolescence. It kept my mind occupied with fun, taught me competition, and served as an outlet for the anger and aggression that would haunt me later. Incidentally, the great Chicago Bears running back, Walter Peyton sent his daughter to Red Pine Camp, primarily because it had such a fantastic reputation.

Campers called my grandma The Duchess because she was always dressed to the nines and demanded good manners and proper decorum, which was especially challenging out in the middle of the woods. She pulled it off beautifully. She was beloved by the campers because she was the one who handed out awards at the end of camp sessions.

She was always very feisty. After Dick passed away, she went to live in a nursing home and even from her wheelchair at 90, she kept everyone on their toes. One time I went to visit her, and she demanded a cigarette. I do not recall her smoking a lot growing up but, by damn when she wanted one, she wanted it right then! She deliberately steered herself around in that wheelchair knocking crap off the tables and bumping into stuff until you gave her one.

Most kids' parents pay good money to send their kids off for a few weeks to swim, waterski and fish; to learn to build a campfire and tell ghost stories; or ramble through the woods looking for rabbits, snakes and insects, but I got it all for free.

When I turned six, they sent me off to Towering Pines Boys Camp for ages up through 11. It was 25 miles from

Red Pines, but it was a blast. From sunup until sundown, I played endless summer sports.

I had a famous bunkmate at Towering Pines named Eric Heiden from Madison, Wisconsin. Eric won five gold medals in speed skating in the 1980 Lake Placid Winter Olympics. I remember him being fast on skates, but I always beat him in tennis.

My mom went to high school with Nancy Heiden, Eric and his sister Beth's mom. When Beth went to Red Pine Camp, she ran three miles a day. She won a bronze Olympic medal for speed skating at the 1980 Lake Placid Winter Olympics, but she won several world championships in women's cycling too. She was also a respectable cross-country skier. I remember trying to get Eric to smoke cigarettes, but he refused because he was training for the Olympics. I have always loved sports, but training for the Olympics takes a special kind of dedication and an amazing level of discipline. I had tremendous respect for both Beth and Eric's commitment.

I went to Towering Pines for five years and spent the next year at Camp Golden Eagle, for older boys, which was just down the road from Red Pines. That was where I started getting more interested in girls than sports and hanging out with the boys.

Dick was the first to recognize after I turned 13 years old, I was spending more time working at the Red Pine Girl's Camp than playing sports and hanging out with the guys at Golden Eagle. I think he got a kick out of watching me flirt for the first time. I probably looked like Opie Taylor trying to stand on his head to impress his girlfriend, Karen on The Andy Griffith Show.

Dick kept me busy washing dishes for 120 campers and 50 staff members, and that chore had to be complete before I could go play football, tennis, basketball or go swimming. So far, I was living every child's envy. How in the world could things go so wrong?

My last year living in Louisiana was also the last year of my innocence in many ways. Up until then, I pretty much kicked everyone's ass in whatever game I played from football to tennis and basketball.

Things all changed when our team, the Gramercy Tigers, played our first game against LaPlace, a town located to the north, across the Mississippi River. I was 13 years old and in 7th grade playing quarterback.

LaPlace brought along the biggest and meanest freaking 7th grade linebacker I have ever seen in my life. Throughout the game, that snorting bull of a boy was either dead center in my face, or knocking me on my ass. All evening, he plowed over our center like a bull out of the chute - with me in his sights. He charged after me with such gleeful ferocity. Several times, I tried to stop him by hurling the football straight into his snarling face mask, but that didn't stop him. He still picked me up off the turf, slammed me to the ground, and finished with a swift kick to my side.

Had our amazing coach, Dr. Monica, not pushed us so hard and accepted no excuses for weakness or failure in both the game and academics, we would not have been tough enough to withstand the viciousness we faced. Because of him, I embraced the brutishness. I relished the rush of adrenaline, always hastening to the thrill and excitement of the fight, and I delighted in the fun of it all.

But more than anything, I took pride in the most excruciating pain I ever experienced in my years of playing sports. Some people call it "sweet pain" born out of passion, but if I am honest, I ran for my life all that night and moved in slow motion for days afterward.

Homecoming that year brought new fantasies and harsh realities about my father to the surface. It happened during the opening ceremonies of the big homecoming football game, when questions about my own father came rushing to the forefront.

It was a cool, starry fall night under the bright stadium lights, the steady drum beat of the high school bands and the aroma of popcorn and baked pretzels coming from the concession stand. As each individual player was introduced, that player walked to midfield alongside their father while the rest of the family cheered and waved from the bleachers.

I loved Dick, but out of no fault of his own, he couldn't be there. So, it was up to me to walk out onto that field by myself.

I was miserable. My fatherlessness fell like a penalty flag on the field at my feet and I was the one who had to pay for whatever mistake had been made that left me without one.

For everyone else and their families, it was a celebratory moment, a picture-perfect memory to be passed down to their children's children. For me, it was a long, lonely walk that felt like a Band-Aid had been ripped off a gaping wound too early, oozing and bleeding onto the field with every step I took.

Instead of making memories, I had been forced to lay bare all my weakness, all my pain, all my shame in front of a lot of happy, cheering people who seemed to me, to have fathers to spare. Why couldn't they lend one to me? Did every person in the world have a father but me?

Wherever he was, did he have any idea how humiliating that night was for me? Shouldn't he have known that his son, who would surely follow in many of his footsteps one day, envision a time when he had to walk out onto a basketball or tennis court, a baseball diamond or football field all alone while his teammates stood proudly with their fathers?

I had considered all angles. Maybe he was incapacitated, locked away in an asylum for the insane, or maybe he was in prison! Worse, perhaps he was dead? I doubted he was deceased. That would have been an easy if not painful explanation for Mom to give. Instead, she refused to talk about it. Regardless of the circumstances, I had to know and after homecoming night, I was committed to demanding answers. I guess she felt I was too young to understand, but answers were coming sooner rather than later, and they came amidst family upheaval.

Except for getting sober after eight years of almost nonstop drinking, our family's permanent move from Louisiana to Wisconsin when I was in the 8th grade would prove to be the most significant and challenging transition of my life.

Located in the north central part of the state of Wisconsin, Minocqua is called the "Island City" where the nation finds recreation on Lake Minocqua. As it turns out, the name "Minocqua" comes from an Ojibwe Indian word meaning "noon-day rest". It was a thriving fishing town, but it was decidedly not a booming metropolis for young people.

Dick and The Duchess retired. Dick would spend all his time trout fishing and he and my grandma were champion bridge players, so they played a lot more bridge. My mom and ReRe took over directorships at Red Pine Camp. Dick gave ReRe the property at Red Pine Camp to build a house and we moved into my grandparents' house at the camp just outside the town of Minocqua.

I was 13 and had been surrounded by assertive female figures most of my life. I loved my mother, sister and ReRe, but for some reason I thought I would be able to assert some authority now that I was a teenager - the young man of the house. I considered myself too old for spankings, groundings and being forced to do anything I didn't want to do. I saw it as a major accomplishment, a rite of passage where the world begins to respond to your commands, and I could finally formulate my own ideas and opinions about things. The older generation has really screwed things up and now I do not have to do what they say. I have my own way.

However, once I turned 13, it didn't take long to realize becoming a teenager was not all it was cracked up to be. I was no longer a little kid, and the adults no longer treated me like a kid. They still ordered me around but there were now expectations, I was supposed to be responsible for my actions and follow rules without argument. This was part of becoming a man. There were other issues that made the transition more difficult as well.

Pubescent hormones were bombarding me like slow-moving neutrons to an atomic bomb. Everything from the cracking of my voice to the sudden widening of my shoulders, to this burst of growth in my hands and feet that didn't match the growth of the rest of my body. It affected how I played sports. I was stronger, faster and nimbler. But I often felt like a freak.

I could not articulate it at the time, nor was I even outwardly aware of how all this was affecting me, but I felt more intensely than ever that I really needed a fatherly figure in my life to explain all this to me. I needed a dad, my dad, to get me through it.

Slowly, over the last year in Lutcher after my slow walk to what felt like the gallows at homecoming, Mom had begun to share little tidbits about mine and Robin's father, Wayne Rolley.

We knew for instance he was a drinker – Mom called him an alcoholic, but we did not inherently understand the ramifications of that. He was remarried, lived in Oklahoma City and was a salesman for an electronics company.

Mom tried to make us understand the extent of the emotional pain she underwent due to his actions; how difficult it had been not having him to help her financially and to make the best decision for us kids; but for Robin and I that was a time so long ago and outside our purview it may as well have been right after the disappearance of the dinosaurs.

For a while she thought she could blot him out from mine and Robin's life, thereby shielding us from his alcoholism. She was not prepared, however, for two children who would eventually want to know more about their father. She had gone to great lengths to postpone that inevitability for as long as possible.

According to my mom, when my sister Robin and I were toddlers, my father decided to move back to Kansas from Milwaukee to go back to school. There was nothing wrong with that, and she said she was always open to working out a plan to make it happen. His heavy drinking, however, complicated things. It was a heavy burden on her and left many emotional scars, which she never quite recovered from. Neither did she forgive him for the difficulties that he was responsible imparting to our family.

My mom worked very hard, and depended on her parents to help raise Robin and I. For most of my childhood, she busted her butt to make sure we had everything we needed. It wasn't easy for her, but the jig was up. I had no anger toward Mom, but I would no longer be deterred. I wanted to see and judge for myself.

Studies say that depression and social anxiety make people more susceptible to alcoholism. I have no doubt that I inherited my father's "alcoholic genes," and that made me what my AA sponsor, Charles Edson called a "thoroughbred alcoholic." Add the emotional pain and Mom's secrecy concerning our heritage, and we were vulnerable.

Mom didn't intentionally want to hurt us, in fact she thought she was protecting us. She knew instinctively that whichever parent is not around to discipline us, to tell us no, and make us do the chores and eat our vegetables would naturally be the parent with whom we would be most drawn. The one who had never been the bad guy, even if technically they were the bad guy, will be the most fascinating, the most fun parent. Mom would be at a great disadvantage with my dad in our lives. She did not want to deal with it, but unfortunately she was about to have to.

While I was adjusting to my new surroundings, I noticed how much independence seemed to be the currency of adolescence. Many of the kids at school were already drinking and smoking pot, influenced by their new friends and a budding sense of rebellion against small-town monotony.

By high school, it seemed like most teens were hanging out after school (and late at night) with their chosen crowd. They often rebelled against adolescence, doing everything they could to make their parents second-guess the joy of having children. They found comfort in each other, bemoaning their homework and pop quizzes, house rules, whether to "go all the way" with their current steady girlfriend or boyfriend, the minutiae of small-town living, and their desire to conquer the world—if only their parents would let them do so.

They found a way to escape all that alleged cruelty by drowning themselves in cheap beer purchased with fake IDs and smoking weed bought from the town's most notorious drug dealers. That rebellion against authority, especially my mother's house rules, seemed to come out of nowhere. But that was probably because I wasn't one to hang around for family night. Sometimes Mom dropped me off at school, but most of the time I had to ride a snowmobile about a mile to reach the highway where I could catch the school bus.

Once out of the house, I played basketball or tennis every day until after dark, so I wasn't as tuned in to the social dynamics swirling around me. Besides, I was busy dealing with my own issues. I had spent a lot of time in Wisconsin, but it had always been for summer visits. The weather was so cold during the winter, I even felt it in my young bones. It's no wonder older people are confined to their rocking chairs and cardigan jackets, sitting in front of roaring fires for nine months with crocheted blankets on their laps. Meanwhile, it's the teenagers who are expected to chop the wood, build the fires, and keep the embers burning—not to mention shoveling snow to clear the sidewalks and driveway.

It took me a while to get used to driving a snowmobile. People said it was easier to follow in the snowmobile tracks of other sledders, but there were no others where we lived. The brakes on a snowmobile aren't that great, and since I had never ridden a motorcycle, I had to learn how to lean into turns. Depending on how hard packed the snow and ice are, you must keep both skis level because it is easy to fall off the sled... believe me, I know.

Then there was the change in dialect from deep southern and Cajun to a mixture of midland and north central that was quite different. The kids often teased us about it. However, if I'm being honest, our new life wasn't all bad.

I learned how breathtaking the snow could be if you looked at it as something other than a bone-chilling hindrance. It inspired me to learn how to snow ski, and that sport was exhilarating! You can fly down slopes and hills at breakneck speeds, weaving in and out between trees. In that instant with the adrenaline pumping, I forgot how hand and feet-numbingly cold it was.

As an aside, though it may seem unimportant, ever since the pain I experienced getting my teeth knocked out, I hated going to the dentist. But our family dentist in Minocqua was a former athlete with another generation of stud athletes around my age. James Francis "Doc" Hartzheim had had a dental practice in Minocqua for over 40 years. He was famous for his "whistle-while-you-work" attitude towards dentistry.

His son Peter was an All-American wrestler at UW-Whitewater, and his daughter Mary was an All-American in track and cross country at UW-Madison. Their daughter Ann was one of my classmates at Lakeland High School. I remember the whole family as great contributors to the community, and I didn't mind going to the dentist with him.

Once again, my ebullient personality and ability to make people laugh, along with being good at sports, aided in the neutralization of what some experts predicted would be just another destabilizing effect of being uprooted. I ran on the cross-country team and continued to play tennis and basketball. We did not have an official tennis team because we did not have a tennis coach, but we did have a basketball team.

On the subject of basketball, I was 4'10" as an 8th Grader, and the best guard on the team. There was a guy named David Meade who was a year older than me and didn't play in high school until his senior year, but he became a staple at Minocqua Park and Recreation where we also played tennis. He was a natural center at 6' 7".

One evening during a raucous game of pickup basketball at the park, I took advantage of our height difference, slipped underneath and stole the ball from him, then scored on a lay-up.

"Hey, what are you, a midget?" Dave razzed me.

"No. What are you, a circus freak?" I taunted back.

I nicknamed him Super Dave. We became the best of friends and remain so to this day, 40 years later. I stood up at his wedding and he stood up at mine, 17 years ago. Super Dave's family had moved to Minocqua from Bluffton, Indiana and Dave's dad Ralph started a small business called A and 1 Electric. Ralph was 6'4" and Dave's mom Anita, was 5'3". They had a huge family, and I adopted all of them as my own including his three brothers Steve, Mike, and Donnie; and two sisters Debbie and Kathy who was killed in an unfortunate accident that devastated the family. Donnie would later play a big part in helping me navigate some difficult family dynamics.

When tensions at home began to escalate, it became too much for my mom. Whenever someone broke house rules or went out all weekend, the quarreling and uncertainty weighed heavily on her. The strain affected me too. I loved my mom and hated to see her in so much distress.

One night, after a particularly chaotic weekend, there was an argument. Mom's frustration boiled over. "I will not allow drinking and smoking weed in this house!" she yelled. "I will not tolerate disappearing for days on end and my not knowing where you are! This is my house, and I have rules for a reason!"

Then, almost as if it were an afterthought, she said, "You need to leave. Go live with your father if that's the life you want, but you won't live like that under my roof!"

Those words hit me hard—not because of the argument itself but because Mom's frustration led her to suggest sending someone to live with my father. That shocked me.

"I want to go too!" I cried impulsively.

"No," she snapped. "I will not expose you to the life your father leads."

Over the next few days, Mom remained visibly troubled. Her outburst had seemed like an act of desperation, but there was also a sense of resolve behind it. Despite the tension, I couldn't stop thinking about visiting my father. I pleaded with Mom, and after a lot of back-and-forth, we came to a compromise: when school let out for summer, she agreed to let me visit him for ten days.

When summer finally arrived, I was a bundle of nerves and excitement. I was finally going to meet the man who had been such a mystery to me all my life.

My first airplane flight was surreal. As I disembarked in Oklahoma City, I immediately scanned the waiting crowd for the man who had been described to me—6'2", good-looking, athletic, just like me. It would turn out to be my first disappointment, although it didn't register as such at the time. Every relationship has its warning signs, but I was young and naïve enough to believe he'd be just as excited to meet me as I was to meet him after twelve years. That proved not to be the case.

He was late. Very late. If it occurred to me that we weren't on the same playing field, I let it go. Instead, I spent the time sitting in the Oklahoma City airport imagining whether he'd recognize me, whether I'd instinctively know him when I saw him. Lost in my fantasies, I suddenly felt a tap on my shoulder.

"Hello, I'm Wayne Quinby Rolley. How you doin' buddy?"

I turned and looked at my father for the first time. It gave me a visible start. I am not sure he noticed, but he did not look anything like the man my mom described. I was looking for a 6' 2" former athlete from whom I received my own athletic build. What I was facing was a 5' 7" hunchback who looked closer to 57 than 37.

Quietly I asked myself, 'Who is *this* guy?'

The reason it so shocked me was because I was not made aware that this man, this father I had never known, was ill with a debilitating disease. He suffered from inflammatory arthritis of the spine known as *ankylosing spondylitis*. The disease, also known as *axial spondyloarthritis*, had over time caused the bones and vertebrae in his spine to fuse together, decreasing his flexibility and ability to stand up straight. The condition caused a distinctively hunched posture. In addition to the pain resulting from the spondylitis, there were concerns it would spread to his ribs, causing an obstruction to his breathing. He was already having difficulty taking deep breaths.

My dad's physical condition was serious, and he said there was no cure. However, he had heard about treatment available at the Mexican College of Rheumatology. It consisted of a mixture of non-steroidal anti-inflammatory drugs called NSAIDs with physical therapy and exercise. It has in several cases significantly slowed down the encumbering progress of the disease. He was working with his doctor to get an appointment at a clinic in Mexico City where he would undergo the relatively experimental treatment. He explained to me he sometimes reached such an excruciating level of pain, he felt he had nothing to lose.

Looking at him, I was saddened for his condition, but it did not restrain my happiness at finally getting to know him. It was cool, I thought, to have him ask questions about my life, school, my friends, whether I had a girlfriend, what foods I liked. On the other hand, my most memorable moments with him were those related to our shared love for athletics. We really hit it off talking about sports and my growing interest in basketball and tennis. Despite his infirmity, he could still throw a football, so we tossed it around the field and held fake wrestling bouts.

"How good are you at basketball?" he asked me one day.

"I'm fast. I've been playing since I was a little kid," I boasted. "I'm a guard at John Curtis Christian. Bet I can beat you at a game of Horse," I challenged him.

"Where did you learn to talk trash?" he asked.

"All my buddies do it," I said.

"It's alright to be cocky if you can back it up. You just better be sure you can!"

Later that afternoon, I beat him three games straight. Afterward, Doreen gave me a hug.

"Your dad loves you Grant," she said reassuringly. "He talks about you all the time."

Her words surprised me considering he hadn't seen me in 12 years. My visit revealed a distinctly different way of life compared to living with Mom. The house rules here were almost nonexistent - behaviors that would have been strictly forbidden at home were tolerated as long as they stayed within the house. It felt like the perfect way to justify bad behavior without really acknowledging it as bad.

I knew somewhere deep down that my dad wasn't going to win any Father of the Year awards, but what kid, accustomed to living under strict rules, wouldn't feel a sense of freedom in such an open environment? And then there was the proverbial elephant in the room. It didn't take long after I arrived to figure out that Mom was right about my dad having a drinking problem. The thing was, Doreen seemed to have one just as bad, if not worse, than his.

They had not been married for long, but Doreen pounded down a half gallon of vodka before lunch every day and my dad stayed up until 3 a.m. every morning drinking it like it was water. I was naïve but I was wise enough to think, 'Wow! They drink a lot!' I excused it as a way for him to cope with the pain of his disease, but the problem did not go unnoticed.

I know now, of course, after going through alcohol addiction myself in the rapidly approaching future, it was actually the other way around. When he and my mom were married, he drank but he did not have spondylitis. There is no known cause of the disease, but research shows it may be a mixture of genetics and the environment. The genetics may have been iffy, but his environment had been one of heavy alcohol consumption for a very long time.

Over the more than 10 days I spent with him, I found him to be grumpy, even churlish, but I would catch flashes of aged good looks and the remnants of athleticism that had to have been attractive to my mom 15 years ago.

He pulled out his old high school scrapbook and I had fun looking through pictures of him during his high school and collegiate sports career. He was a talented athlete in his day and attended the University of Kansas where he met my mom and Wilt Chamberlain who was there when he was. Whether it was wrestling, basketball or football, he left me with a spattering of heartwarming moments I remember to this day.

CHAPTER 3:

BREAKING POINT

"Young man are you a thoroughbred alcoholic?" asked the tall man wearing a cowboy hat who approached me shortly after attending my first AA meeting in 1980. He had swagger, a wealthy international businessman who told it like it was, Charles Edson was my first and only AA sponsor. I immediately liked him and trusted him, but I had no idea what he meant.

"I don't know what that means, but I have drunk enough to get me here," I told him honestly. I was on my second drug and alcohol rehabilitation stint, but it was my first trip to an AA meeting.

A thoroughbred alcoholic is a person who comes from a long, established line of alcoholism and who must be willing to fight all the odds to overcome it because it is imbedded in your genes.

"I am a recovered thoroughbred alcoholic," he responded. "A lot of people will tell you, just like they did me, you cannot overcome it; that you will always crave alcohol; that it is a battle you will fight to a stalemate, but never really win.

"I'm here to tell you that if you do everything I say and follow the rules laid out in AA's Big Book," he continued, "you can and will recover while the rest of these sons of bitches live out the rest of their lives *trying* to recover.

"I like the way you talk and handle yourself, Mr. Edson," I said, and I meant it.

According to the National Institute on Alcohol Abuse and Alcoholism, genetics influence about 50 percent of alcohol addiction, but it isn't the only factor. The environment in which one lives is also at play.

I started drinking at age 14 and served my first stint in rehab by the time I turned 19. After that, I was sober for three months until I made my first mistake of thinking I could handle it. At 23, I woke up handcuffed to a bed in a rehab in Ft. Lauderdale. After that, with the help of my AA counselor, Tom Dugdale, and Charles, my sponsor - neither of whom ever pulled any punches - I made up my mind to become a healthy, productive member of society. I got clean and sober by age 24 and I have not looked back in over four decades. But that makes it sound much too easy. It is not easy at all.

I have described my fight with alcohol as going 15 rounds in a boxing match. You wake up one morning with a horrendous hangover and you say, no way I want to feel like this. I can beat it! But then, you bounce back the next day, so you drink again. You try to hold your punches this time, but before you know it, the liquor has knocked you out again. Alcohol is a formidable opponent. One part of your brain says of course you can beat the booze, but another part of your brain says no, you're going to lose.

The late legendary basketball coach Bobby Knight once said 'No' is the most important word you will ever learn. "No, I don't"; "No, I won't"; "No, I can't» – they all make a lot of sense in the context of things that are not good for you.

"The mental is to the physical as four is to one" he said regarding the importance of mental toughness. I would have loved to have played for him, and I quote him often while teaching myself.

I am one of the fortunate ones. I came to accept something alcoholics must come to terms with but often don't. We can't drink - ever. After a long period of drinking, your brain begins to rely on alcohol to produce certain chemicals. This is what makes it difficult for thoroughbred drinkers to quit.

Upon returning home, I had a newfound outlook on family. I had a father who called me every Sunday to talk. He asked about my week, about my tennis matches and my relationship with my coach. He seemed to enjoy talking about athletics and hearing about my competitive spirit.

After those 10 unforgettable days, I became more aware, if that was even possible, of other kids playing football with their dads. I had craved that opportunity most of my life and now I could claim it as my own.

Less than a month after I got home, he called to tell me he had received approval from his doctor to check into the Reumatologia Clinica in Mexico City to undergo the NSAIDS treatment. I wished him well, knowing I probably wouldn't hear from him for a few days. It didn't matter. We had plenty of time to explore this new and novel relationship.

I also became more aware of the things about him I wanted to adopt as my own, to make me more of my father's son and to show everyone how much like my dad I really was.

When I got back home, I wanted to make some money in case I had the opportunity to go see my dad again. I brainstormed an idea for getting a job mowing lawns. I even had a clever marketing approach. I used the telephone book to look up single women.

In those days, phone numbers were listed by their last name and usually the married residents had "Mr. and Mrs." after that. If they were single, it would be their last name, first name. It worked most of the time.

"I have some awesome news," I said into the receiver when a lady inevitably answered the phone. "I'll bet you need someone to mow your lawn and rake your leaves. Guess what, I'm here to help you with that!"

I started working consistently within days of being back, making excellent money for a young guy. Again, my gregarious personality kept them entertained on the side with jokes and a little flirtation. The ladies brought me cold drinks and sometimes told me how cute I was. I was on Cloud Nine.

We also had a group of guys at Lakeland High who played tennis at Minocqua Parks and Recreation. I approached school leadership about starting a tennis team, but they said, "No. We don't have a coach, nor do we have the budget to hire one."

Without a coach we didn't have any formal teaching, and I was upset by the rejection, but I had proven myself proficient at selling stuff on the telephone. All we needed to start a tennis team was six people so I easily found six guys I knew would be interested. I put on a deep voice and called a bunch of schools and said we were in the process of starting a tennis team and we were looking for opponents. Before I knew it, we had an intramural tennis team, and we arranged to play on the parks and recreation courts. I set up six matches and I bought a new tennis racket for good luck.

I had just returned home from winning our first match and I was out on the back deck practicing my backhand when I heard the telephone ring inside. A few minutes later, my mom came to the door and asked me to come inside because she had something to tell me.

"What?" I asked. I don't think I had ever seen Mom that serious before.

"Grant," she said in a melancholy tone. "I have some bad news, honey."

"What's wrong, Mom?"

"It's your father, Grant. He has passed away."

All I remember after that was smashing my new tennis racket to pieces against the deck railing.

CHAPTER 4:

GAME OF MISTAKES

Ten days. Four Sunday phone calls and ten days of fun were all I had with my dad before he died. My mom explained he was on his way to Mexico City for the new treatments, but he never made it. Doreen rushed him to a Phoenix hospital after he fell ill during a layover. What's more, his death was not a result of the disease, but from complications with alcoholism.

Mom and I attended the funeral together. I had never been to a funeral before, and now I was attending my dad's. It was hard for me to wrap my head around his death. This was the dad I had dreamed about all my life, and now he was gone at only 37 years old - just weeks after I finally met him. I couldn't get over the fact that I had finally renewed my long-awaited relationship with him, only for it to end so suddenly. It left me feeling sad and vulnerable, not to mention even more abandoned than I had felt before meeting him.

I will never forget the week I spent with him. To this day, I wish I had spent more time getting to know him - not just him, but more about his life and his side of the story with Mom. Mom knew I was taking it hard and tried to console me, but I couldn't help but feel bothered by the fact that she never shed a tear over him.

"Did he abuse you, hit you or anything," I asked.

"No, Grant," she responded. "He just never grew up."

I was taken by how well-liked he seemed to be by so many people he worked with and who were his friends. People I did not know came up to me after the service to offer their condolences and tell me how proud he was of me. Afterwards, the pain was like a tsunami, rumbling in my soul and flooding my heart.

Through the years, I have been able to analyze the situation with adult clarity and I see what a coward my dad was. Not only was he a scoundrel for what he did, but he was also selfish, putting himself first and refusing to accept responsibility as a husband and father.

To this day, I don't know if it was a self-destructive streak, whether it was hereditary, or I wanted to test my own fortitude and lost the battle, but I had never experienced that kind of emotional pain and it was so visceral, I felt it physically. And I was angry! I had to find a way to get this anger and pain under control. I didn't know what to do with it.

To set the stage for what was coming, Minocqua is a drinking town, and it had the suds for people at a young age. As an example of how prominent drinking among young people was in Minocqua, one of the best players on the high school basketball team began drinking so heavily, it became an issue for the coaches and the team. By the time I graduated high school, he had committed suicide by stabbing himself in the heart.

Furthermore, of the more than 100 taverns on the island, the Thirsty Whale was by far the most popular. They had a "Bucket Club" where once you drank 20 ounces of liquor, you earned a bucket that you then autographed on the bottom and hung from the ceiling. I became one of its proud young members at age 17.

One night I was in a bar in Minocqua when Barbara Farley, a lady who worked at Red Pine Camp, introduced me to her brother Chris who was sitting at a table with a bunch of girls. Yes, it was the same comedian Chris Farley who would go on to join the cast of Saturday Night Live.

Of course, he was not famous then, so I asked him what he did for a living.

"I am a scuba diving instructor at Camp Red Arrow for Boys," he said. "I get stoned and sink to the bottom and exhale by blowing bubbles to the surface."

The class clown cannot be undone, so I walked up to him later and started pouring beer in my ear.

Chris gave me a high-five and said, "I like that shit. When did you come up with that?"

"Just now." I turned to the girls who were with him and said, "It goes into the bloodstream faster through the ear, so I'll get drunk faster and have enough money left over to buy you breakfast after you spend the night with me."

After that, I became rather famous in Minocqua as the guy who drank beer through his ear.

Super Dave became like a big brother I never had. We were always hanging out and caterwauling at the girls. He and I formed a tight-knit group of buddies that included Richard Simmons, Brian Tapp, Scott Petrowski, and Jerry Clawson who was nicknamed Grizz.

We saw ourselves as bad-asses, Minocqua's own Dukes of Hazard, daring and adventurous, well-meaning and basically honest, but very mischievous. We were part pranksters and part gangsters.

One night after a game of pickup football, Grizz pulled up to the field with three cases of beer. At the time, Grizz and Dave were only 16, and I was just 14. I had never tasted alcohol before, though the older boys had a reputation for getting buzzed after every game. Several of my friends were already drinking, and they always seemed to be having a great time.

He looked funny lugging cases of beer, so I laughed and said, "Hey Grizz! Where did you get all that beer!"

Grizz broke off a six-pack and pitched it to me. "Start pounding, Rolley. You can't get drunk on beer."

Unfortunately, I believed him.

After several weeks, beer after football became a ritual. Then after tennis, and then after softball, and then after basketball. The theory was, we would get together as often as possible after school to play a few games and drink for the buzz, since you 'couldn't get drunk on beer'.

That first day of drinking, I had three cans of beer and to be honest, I did not immediately like the taste, but I took quickly to that first euphoric buzz. It was fun.

The next time we drank, I had five cans. By the time I was a senior in high school, I was drinking a 12-pack at a sitting, and by the time I got to college, it was easily a case.

I had no idea I had just started down the road to alcoholism, and that I was what Charles characterized as a thoroughbred alcoholic. The alcoholism genes ran through my father's side of the family, and it had nothing to do with self-control, endurance, or pain. It was all about having a high susceptibility for alcohol addiction.

Rather than stopping after the nice little buzz I got from my first two or three beers, it triggered a chemical reaction that made it nearly impossible on a normal level to stop. I ignored the fact that at some point, the effects are reversed. If three gave me a happy buzz, then six will give me twice the happy buzz, and if six didn't do it, 12 would.

My main problem was not that I drank all day. It was that whatever time of day I started drinking, I couldn't quit. That made me an alcoholic.

Drinkers of all ages are unprepared for alcohol dependency and addiction, but unfortunately, life was already clearing a path for me to rehab with quick stops along the way for cocaine and other illicit drugs.

Even worse, throughout high school, my drinking increased. There were endless parties every weekend and everything we did as a group of friends revolved around drinking. Whether it was camping, fishing, or playing athletic games, cases of beer were involved.

My buddy Richard Simmons was one of my favorite tennis opponents and his parents, as I mentioned earlier, owned Bethels Bar. Bethels was the sponsor for our intramural softball, basketball, and tennis teams at the city park and it was in support of Bethels that Super Dave started his Goofy Golf tournament.

Dave was a great sports coordinator. Although basketball was his favorite sport, he also played golf, tennis and softball recreationally. He started what we called the Dope Open in tennis and ran a Goofy Golf tournament to support the Bethel's Bar intramural softball team, which still exists today.

By now we are all legal age to buy and drink responsibly so Bethels gave us unlimited access to beer before and after games. Richard and I would start out with a station wagon loaded with an iced-down case of beer compliments of Bethels. We usually won all six matches, then celebrated by drinking all the way home. If you grew up in the 1970s, you probably remember the teary-eyed Indian public service announcements on TV, asking people not to litter.

He must have boohooed out loud as we tossed our empty beer cans and bottles out the window.

Within a few weeks of my beer drinking, we ended up at Richard's house doing shots. We had moved beyond a 'non-drunk' beer buzz and graduated into getting stump-stumbling, mind-numbingly sloshed.

That marked the beginning of my partying days, but we didn't smoke cigarettes or weed. Super Dave said true athletes didn't smoke and I still think he was right about that, even though later in a boozy haze, I started smoking anything anyone offered me.

From there, it didn't take me long to start hitting the taverns.

I have mentioned how difficult it was for me to sit through class. I could not sit still but now I had booze to help me get through the day. Bethels was two blocks down the street from Lakeland High School, so I began leaving school during break periods and doing quarter shots of beer for an hour or two, going back to school with a buzz, and returning after school to go off and play games with the boys and drink more.

I would have said then I was drinking to bury pain, but really - what pain? It was illogical. I grew up without a father. I was old enough to realize that many boys grow up without fathers and some for much more tragic reasons. I was not completely without a male mentor. My grandfather Dick did the best he could to teach me and guide me through hard times when I was a little boy, and Dave's dad Ralph treated me like a member of the Meade family. Shouldn't I be grateful I was not alone, isolated, without friends and family that loved me? I was not abused, hungry, desolate or running from the law... although it would not be long before I would have encounters with them!

But I didn't think about any of that. My junior year of high school and Dave's senior year, the only year he played high school basketball, I got sidelined after my buddy Scott Petrowski knocked me into a wall during basketball practice and broke my collarbone.

I was furious. "Dammit Scott! Why did you do that?" I yelled at him in pain.

"Sorry Rolley, but I can't give up an easy one," he said.

I continued to do my part for the team by becoming Super Dave's most vociferous and drunkest cheerleader. I egged him on by getting drunk at all the games pounding beer and holding up signs that said, "Feed Meade".

Aside from my successful sneak attack on Dave, he would go on to have a hell of a senior season, breaking Lakeland High's scoring record in basketball with 39 points and setting three of the school's rebound records that remain unbroken today.

All the students were still congratulating Dave in our Monday morning Modern Social Problems class. His feat was so spectacular, even our teacher Mr. Roper, stood up in front of the class and made an announcement.

"I am proud to announce that David Meade has finally made a positive contribution to society. Class dismissed."

Dave got a standing ovation from the class. Despite all the drinking we did together, Dave never had a problem with alcohol, but he bailed my ass out of several potential drunken danger zones.

A couple years after high school graduation, Super Dave and I played in an Upper Peninsula Independent Basketball Association 2 on 2 outdoor basketball tournament in Michigan. Dave was playing for Coach Deke Routheau at Gogebic Community College in Ironwood at the time.

He and I won five games out of the 15 games we played, scoring one point for each basket. There were a couple of teams competing who had players that were 6'5" but Dave still controlled the games.

We were drinking beer on the way home, and stopped at the Bear Bar in Boulder Junction, Wisconsin. All over the walls were these taxidermies of huge animals and birds. It was quite impressive, but I was drunk and my smartass inquiry as to who killed all the animals didn't go over very well.

The bartender said, "I did, bow hunting."

I honestly don't remember exactly what I said but I could be a mouthy drunk and I think I called him Robin Hood.

For those who don't know it, bowhunters consider their sport superior to other means for hunting, especially those using a shotgun or rifle. A bow and arrow are very heavy and hard to pull. It takes a lot of patience and perseverance and strength to steady the aim. The aim must be exact too, to prevent mortally wounding the animal and it's running off to die slowly. Most bowhunters shoot for the heart and try not to miss.

"No, you didn't," I accused. "I don't believe you. You're full of shit!"

He gave me a dirty look. "Hey shit-for-brains, I can shoot an apple off your head at 100 yards for $100 bucks. Wanna try it?"

He handed me an apple and told me to walk until he said stop. For some reason I did it.

"Hey kid," he yelled at my back. "Don't worry. If I miss a little low, you can keep the arrow!"

Suddenly Super Dave appeared between us in his truck spinning gravel. He threw open the car door. "Get in dumb ass!" he yelled, and we took off out of there.

Looking back at those days, Super Dave and I took a lot of road trips, drinking all the way to our destination and all the way back home again. We are very lucky we never had, or was involved in, a car accident or worse, although there was that one time.

It was late at night. I had agreed to stay awake to help keep him awake too, but I was nodding off. He reached over and slapped me upside the head.

"Wake up asshole!" he said and about that time, he lost control of the wheel as we hit some gravel and we did a 360° circle in the middle of the road, just barely missing a passing car. Ever since that night, I have believed fervently in guardian angels. That woke me up for sure but unfortunately, there were too many nights like that. I thank God nothing serious ever happened. It's a miracle, really.

Everything changed after I started drinking, but there were still a lot of good things happening that would have a positive effect on my life long-term. I was playing so much tennis, I stopped running cross country to play more. The difference? I played every tennis match hungover and often on speed, and I still won a lot.

Impressed by my ability and initiative at forming the tennis team and coordinating tennis matches, the park director hired me to teach kids tennis at the park during the summer. They paid me .50 per student per lesson and I built up a lot of students, eventually making between $15 and $20 per day. I was amped up!

One of my students was Steve "Pork" Rosholt, the 12-year-old son of one of our local bankers and commercial developers. Marti Rosholt built Timber Ridge Country Club, an 18-hole golf course with four tennis courts in Oneida County.

Pork won the Wausau Open in the Boys 12 division after working with me. Afterwards, Marti hired me as the Tennis

Pro at his new club during the summer. It was a great opportunity, but because I was so young and because of my drinking, I made every possible mistake while working there. The Rosholt family eventually moved to Scottsdale, Arizona and Pork got a full ride to Northwestern where he became an All-State running back in football.

One day after winning a match at the park, a member of the opposing team approached me.

"Why don't you guys jump on the tournament circuit and start sanctioning tournaments for rankings?" he asked. "You guys are good enough."

I didn't know anything about the tournament circuit, but I checked it out and found one in Manitowoc, Wisconsin, three hours away. My mom bought me a bus ticket, but I cashed it in and hitchhiked to Manitowoc with my sleeping bag. The guy who picked me up asked where I was going. When I told him, Black Hawk Park for a tennis tournament, he invited me to stay at his house.

When I arrived, his daughter was having a keg party for graduation, and I was invited. I got drunk and the next day, the family watched me play the No. 6 seed, a boy in Wisconsin in the boys 16 age group. I lost 6-4, 6-4 and the dad drove me back to Wausau. Even though I lost, I learned to play with better players.

As they say, you win some and you lose some. I took some losses, but I won more than I lost. After winning a match during one tournament, a spectator approached me afterward and asked me my name and how old I was.

"Grant Rolley. I'm fourteen," I said.

"You realize you could win this tournament, don't you?"

I thought I was pretty good. It came natural to me like so many other sports, so I was flattered and encouraged by his words. But I was not at that time overly confident because I had no formal training or tournament play experience, so I demurred.

"Oh, I don't know. That last guy was easy to beat, but I don't know if the rest will be so easy," I said.

"That last guy is a cake eater, like so many tennis players out here on the circuit," he said.

Okay, I'll bite. "What is a cake eater?"

"Rich, self-indulgent, selfish. Probably took lessons but has little natural talent," he said. "In other words, a wimp."

I never knew that man's name, but I never forgot that lesson and through the years I discovered he was right. There are a lot of wealthy people who play tennis. They can afford to belong to a club with a tennis following, they can afford to take lessons, afford to buy all the most expensive rackets, wear all the designer gear, and they think that makes them good at the game.

"There are players, and there are hitters in tennis," the man continued.

I wondered why he had picked me out to share these nuggets of wisdom. "Young man, you are a player. That guy you just beat is overconfident. He looks good hitting on the court, but he can't play. That's why you beat him."

If my dad thought I was talking smack in basketball, he hadn't seen anything after the confidence this man instilled in me at a young age. I not only trash talked, I learned to hustle too, hanging around the courts.

One day when I was still in high school at Lakeland, I was playing a guy named John Blumenstein when another guy pulled up in a Mercedes Benz convertible. His name was Hamed Ali, and he asked me who was the best tennis player at the park.

"That man right there," I said pointing to John, the man I was currently playing. "John Blumenstein is the best. I bet you $20 John will beat you in a match," I said.

Ali won easily and proceeded to brag about how good he was.

"Tell you what," I said in response to his boasting. "I'll bet you $300 I can kick your ass on the court."

I didn't have $300, but John was not that good. I beat him all the time and after watching Ali play John and win, I was certain I could beat him, and I did.

Ali called me out for 'setting him up to lose', but he then took me to the famous Little Bohemia Lodge for beers.

Located in Manitowish Waters, Wisconsin, Little Bohemia is the site of a shootout between the FBI and John Dillinger during the early 1930s. Dillinger and his gang escaped but the lodge still has hundreds of bullet holes in its walls. Ali wound up hiring me to play with him the rest of the summer for $15 an hour.

Another time, I met a guy who was practicing blasting serves, and I was so impressed, I introduced myself. His name was Mark Hansen from Atlanta, and he played at Abraham Baldwin Agricultural College in Tifton, Georgia. He had a cottage in Lake Minocqua. He was very good, and we played every day for the rest of the summer. We're still friends to this day.

The Indians may no longer be allowed to scalp people, but it doesn't stop them from threatening and fantasizing about it. We had an interesting, to say the least, relationship with them, both good and bad.

There were four steel reinforced tennis nets at the park where we played. The park left them up all winter but spearfishing was a big sport among the Indians, and they would come to the park and take down the nets and use them to hold fish. It was weird but whenever we went to play and the nets were missing, we would go down to the reservation, take them out of the water, and bring them back, clean them up and set them back on the posts.

One day when we went to get the nets, Richard and an Indian named Larry Mann got into a fist fight over a girl. They were really popping at each other, and it was dragging on for about 10 minutes.

"Hey Richard, need any help?" I yelled over to him as we headed back with the nets.

"Hell no! I don't need any damn help!"

We just left him there fighting and returned with the nets.

That's how it was. It could get rough.

When I turned 16, Mom wanted me to get my driver's license, but we couldn't afford to buy a car, even an old one, so I was indifferent. What good is a license if you don't have a car to drive. It did not slow me down, though. I caught a lot of rides from friends who had a car, and I had adjusted to traveling short distances on a snowmobile. If it was nearby, I would hop on it and meet my friends wherever we were going – school, parties, sporting events or whatever.

Proms, however, where most kids shine up the old jalopy, put on a suit, take a girl out to a nice expensive dinner and get shitfaced drunk, was just not to be for me.

When I was a senior, I invited a girl named Kim to homecoming. She was not someone I was dating, and we were not a couple. We were just friends. She was on the decorating committee for the homecoming dance, and she invited me to come along and help decorate the gymnasium the night before the dance. I was not in the least interested in doing that, so naturally, I went out with my buddies.

Apparently, Kim and a bunch of friends from the committee went out afterward and got drunk. She fell into a lake and skinned her forehead. The next night when I picked her up to take her out to dinner before the dance, she complained she didn't feel well. I still think it was the embarrassment of having a gash on her forehead at the senior prom. That had to be worse even than getting a big pimple on your face, especially for a girl. Anyway, all she ordered was a salad and the dance itself was cut short. My buddies all ragged on me about what a cheap date she was and joked that I was damn lucky she didn't order a steak on my budget.

Super Dave was a legend socially and athletically in school. He had a lot of friends and an entourage of women following him around. Most teachers gave him his due laughter for some of his antics. He had a natural ability to lighten the mood and generate laughter in the shadow of serious circumstances.

One day in Mr. Roper's Modern Social Problems class, me, Rodney Kainer, David Merkle and Super Dave gave a joint oral report on abortion. It was a very 'modern' topic. Nothing since the Civil Rights Act of 1964 and the Vietnam War was more prominent in the news in 1975 than Roe vs. Wade and the legalization of abortion.

In those days, the Supreme Court of the United States was not as polarized and politicized as it is today. Judges were not referred to as Democratic judges or

Republican judges. However, when at least two of the court's justices, Warren Burger and Lewis Powell, Jr. who had been appointed by Republican presidents, sided with the majority Democratic court to decide in a 7-2 decision in favor of legalizing abortion nationwide, Republicans and their allies were not only angry because they were staunchly against abortion, but they questioned the viability of the high court's decision based on an argument of "right to privacy".

Regardless of how brutally charged the topic is today more than 40 years later, it was still acceptable in the 1970s to discuss social issues like abortion, openly and forcefully in high schools, churches, and out in the public square, without the threat of violence and imprisonment.

After our joint presentation, Mr. Roper asked the class, "Does anyone have any questions concerning this report?"

We were 15 and 16-year-olds. It depended on how open your family was about discussing sex as to how much a girl or boy knew about sex. Whether she was genuinely asking a serious question or just playing dumb, I don't know, but a girl in the front row raised her hand and asked, "How does a girl get pregnant?"

"Stay after class for 15 minutes and I will show you," Dave quipped.

It brought the house down. Even Mr. Roper couldn't stifle a laugh.

"Another Super Dave story started when I was a junior and invited to the homecoming prom by a gorgeous classmate, Patty Brown. Patty and I double-dated with Richard Simmons and his date, Stacy—who, ironically, is now married to Super Dave.

I had to drive out to the reservation to pick Patty up, and as if that wasn't nerve-wracking enough, I arrived to discover her father, George Brown, was a Chippewa tribal chief. I got so nervous, I forgot to take a picture—one of those memories you're supposed to hold onto forever, especially for the girl."

Later, several high schoolers from the Chippawa Nation basketball team wanted to recruit 6' 7" Super Dave to play with them in an all-Indian basketball tournament in North Dakota. Chief George Brown made it happen.

At first, Super Dave declined the invite. "I am clearly no Indian!" he argued.

Chief Brown told him, "You are now." He handed Dave Larry Mann's library card as identification. "If anyone asks just say you are an Indian named Larry Mann and show them the card."

"But clearly, I am not an Indian," Dave argued.

"It doesn't matter, say you are an Indian named Larry Mann and show them the library card if they argue," Chief Brown said.

But sure enough, when the team arrived at the tournament venue and Super Dave disembarked from the team passenger van, cries of, "That guy ain't no friggin' Indian!" arose from the opposing team members.

"Surely they can see I'm not an Indian," Dave said to Chief Brown.

"No matter what they say, claim you are an Indian named Larry Mann, and we will back you up," said the chief. "They can't prove you aren't."

The Chippewa made it to the Championship game playing against the Sioux Nation with Dave leading the team in scoring points.

Again, there were complaints, "We just don't believe that mother is an Indian," said one of the Sioux team representatives.

By this time, Dave was really into it.

"Oh yes I am," said Dave. "My name is Larry Mann, and I am an Indian!"

When the coach called Chief Brown to further protest, he said "I have told you four times. His name is Larry Mann, and he is an Indian!" then slammed down the phone.

The Chippewa won a gigantic trophy and Ralph, Dave's dad found him passed out on the kitchen floor the next morning clutching the championship trophy for the Chippawa Nation.

That summer, Dave and I rented a cabin on Mercer Lake in Minocqua for $40 a month. We were both working and were rarely there to enjoy it. At the end of the summer, the owner reminded us we owed him $80, and we paid up. Today, it would cost us $40 a day! No one thought Super Dave and I would amount to anything, but ironically - or perhaps miraculously - Dave and I became the most successful of all the kids from Lakeland Union High School in 1975 and 1976. Dave became a teacher and basketball coach, and I have been a successful tennis player and coach, so as they say – Screw 'em if they can't take a joke!

All Super Dave's family too, have at one time or another, been fantastic friends and they all have a great sense of humor.

Another time, we were out riding around when Mike Meade, Dave's oldest brother suddenly yelled, "Pull over! Quick! Look at that big ass buck!" he yelled. He jumped out and grabbed his bow from the back of the truck and shot twice. The buck was still standing.

My grandfather, Dick had been a forest ranger, I knew all the game wardens in the area, and I saw Frank White pull up behind us. Mike was baffled he had missed twice, and the deer was still just standing there.

"Sorry Mike, but I'm afraid I'll have to give you a ticket," Frank said.

"Why?" Mike asked, beginning to realize something was up.

"For being a rotten shot," he laughed. "And for not realizing that is a decoy."

Another hilarious event was when we were playing an all-Indian baseball team on a reservation in Lac du Flambeau, 15 miles west of Minocqua.

Leroy White hit a fly ball to center field and hit Mike on the head, knocking his cap off and flying over the wall for a home run. The Indians didn't have any stands, they all watched the game from their cars. When Leroy hit the home-run, the Indians started honking their horns and yelling, "Way to use your head, Meade!"

Years later, Steve had a stroke, and the doctor came into his room because there had to be limitations to visitation.

"Mr. Meade, is there anyone specific you don't want us to allow in your room for a visit?"

"Yeah, Barack Obama," Steve blurted.

CHAPTER 5:

OUT OF BOUNDS

As if up to that point, instability had not done enough subliminal damage to my psyche, Mom threw another monkey wrench into the works and pulled me out of Lakeland High School at the beginning of my senior year. I was to spend my last year of high school at an elite prep school called Wayland Academy in Beaver Dam, Wisconsin. I was furious.

"Why! Why are you doing this to me during my senior year?" I fumed. "Who changes schools their senior year?"

"Because you are getting a Social Security check from your father's estate, and I want to use it to ensure you get a good education," my mother said. "I want you to go to college and this will help prepare you for it."

Now I am being forced into subjugation with a bunch of spoiled, rich kids wearing suits and ties to class. I despised school! Of all the things to spend money on that we had never had! How about a car? How about buying herself or Robin something practical? How about some new furniture or athletic shoes and a tennis racket? But school! Honestly, it would not have mattered whether she wanted to send me to Podunk University or Harvard, I was not into school. I only showed up at all so I could play sports.

More than 30 years later, people would explain to me that I clearly have attention deficit and hyperactivity disorder. ADHD is a common but usually chronic condition that starts in childhood and persists into adulthood. During the 1970s there was no name like ADHD for being a bad student. You were either a good one or a bad one and I was a bad one.

As an adult, my ADHD has many times blocked depression from catching up to me, as Charles used to say; but as an adolescent, it meant sitting in a classroom listening to lectures and taking tests and that could not hold my attention. I had to be always moving and doing something.

At 16 years old, I could not rationalize why my mom thought school was an answer to my recklessness. Looking at it now, maybe she believed I was just bored and all I needed was a more challenging school environment to renew my interest in academics. She knew I was not stupid. I was always hanging out with friends and playing sports games, so maybe she was more aware of my drinking than I realized. Perhaps she felt a change would do me good, but if that was her reasoning, Wayland only increased my misbehavior in that regard. There was no arguing with her. I was going off to Wayland like it or not.

Ironically, Wayland Academy turned out not to be all bad. In fact, some very good things came of it, one being they had a school tennis team. Mom helped move me into my dorm room but before heading back to Minocqua, she wanted to tour the campus. One of the first places we stopped was the athletics department.

Coach Sol Wolfe coached tennis, swimming and soccer. He joined the school in 1934, so he had been coaching there for over 40 years by the time I was a senior at Wayland. He was quite the character. His coaching methods would not be allowed in schools today. He was an old-school coach who believed in developing talent and improving performance by pushing his players beyond their own expectations, military-style in many ways. He was a strict disciplinarian who even resorted to threats if it pushed us to be better. He also cursed like a sailor.

"Coach Wolfe, my name is Sarah Rolley, and I want to introduce you to my son, Grant," my mom said. "He is a pretty good tennis player."

"Lady, I have been hearing that from moms for years," he growled. "Sign the boy up."

He winked at me and said, "Come see me once you get settled in."

I did go meet with him a couple days later and he cut me absolutely no slack.

"Do you know what the Continental Grip is?" He handed me a tennis racket off the wall.

I had no idea, so I answered academically.

"The United States?"

"No, numb nuts," he groused. "It's your grip on the racket for serving.

I explained to him I was primarily a basketball player, and Lakeland didn't have a tennis team, so we had formed our own local intramural team, and I had no formal training in tennis at all.

"Your mother said you were good. With no training, how the hell can you be any good?"

I bucked myself up to challenge him. "Because I am smart. I have played a lot of sports all my life and I have an instinct that helps me anticipate shots, I can think on my feet. I can solve problems," I assured him. "Really and truly, Coach Wolfe, I am probably a better overall athlete than anybody here at this school."

"We'll see," he said doubtfully and walked off leaving me standing there to think about how I could prove it to him.

I played football, basketball and tennis at Wayland. I did not play soccer or swim, but many times I watched Coach Wolfe work the swimmers. He made them practice in the first lane so he could crawl alongside them on the edge of the pool yelling, "Breathe you son of a bitch, breathe!"

I knew instinctively I needed his kind of authoritative father figure in my life, and I didn't mind that he bitched at me a lot. He was a tough guy and hated to lose, and I respected his tactics. It worked on me, and I grew to love the guy. He would turn out to be the best tennis coach I ever had.

"I want you to sit in your dorm room with a tennis ball and volley off the wall using this Continental Grip until you get comfortable with it," he told me that first day. "Come back when you feel you are ready to play with it."

Coach Wolfe eventually acknowledged I had some natural athletic ability for tennis.

"Where did you get that innate ability to trash talk?" he asked me one day. If that sounds familiar, my dad had asked me the same thing just a few years back.

"I grew up playing sports against Chippewa Indians."

I explained that in 8th grade, I was beating an Indian opponent at basketball when he threatened to scalp me if I made another basket.

"I learned you had to talk shit to compete against some of those guys. They were tough guys," I told Coach Wolfe.

That was also how I met my best friend Super Dave, talking smack on the basketball court. Then he went on to explain the facts of tennis life to me.

"If an opponent in tennis is 25 percent better than you, you cannot win," he said. "If they are 10 percent better, it is possible to make up the difference by being in better physical condition, having mental toughness and tenacity - all that," he continued. "But the only way you can beat somebody significantly better than you is to get into their hemisphere, mess with their mind. You are natural at that. Keep doing it."

That little tidbit upheld me most of my career. The only time it was a detriment was over 30 years later when my friend Dan Lucas, whom I met at River Chase Country Club in Hoover, Ala. where he was the tennis pro, first nominated me for the Alabama Sports Hall of Fame.

People tried to warn me, "Grant, you are not going to get in."

I asked why.

"Because you are not very nice when you play," they said.

"I do not play to make friends," I always responded.

But they were right as usual.

A woman on the Board of Directors and selection committee said she had watched me play and I smashed three rackets over the post. She voted against me, and I did not get in that year.

Late in the semester, Coach Wolfe said to me, "Grant, I'm going to do you a big favor. You don't have to go to biology class anymore. I got you out of it."

I was thrilled. "Fantastic!"

"You are a shitty student Grant," – there it was again. "But you are going farther in tennis than you ever will dissecting a damn frog."

That same year, I made it to the state finals. My mom and ReRe made the trip to Appleton for the match. We won the first set 6-4, lost the second set 6-4, and we were down 4-1 in the third set.

During a mandatory 120 second break, Coach Wolfe was not happy with my sporadic play. "Listen you son of a bitch. If you miss one more service return, I'm going to tell the headmaster you have a laundry bag full of empty beer bottles and half pints of Yukon Jack in the bottom of your closet in your dorm room. What do you think about that? You know what that means don't you, no diploma!"

I was stunned. "H-h-h-how do you know that?" I stammered.

"First of all, you just told me dumb shit, but second of all, I know everything about you." Then he gave me a sinister grin that sent fear tingling down my backside. "Now, get your shit together."

We won six games in a row and took home the title. Coach Wolfe hugged me afterward and warned me to watch my boozing, but his threats remained on repeat for the rest of my term at Wayland.

One afternoon, I went to watch him coach the soccer team. From the sidelines I heard him yell across the field, "Kick it out of the damn zone!"

The headmaster just happened to be watching too, and when he heard Coach Wolfe raising hell, he shouted just as loud, "Shut the hell up, Wolfe!"

He had been at Wayland 42 years, and everybody loved him and overlooked his vulgarity because he was such an effective coach, and his teams were made for the Wayland Academy record books. They won 14 conference championships and one state championship in swimming under his tenure as coach.

In 2022, Coach Wolfe was inducted into the Wayland Athletic Hall of Fame. His coaching record was part of his bona fides. As for his personal accolades, he had 16 varsity letters before graduating from Wayland himself in 1934. After college, he was drafted by the Detroit Lions but returned to Wayland in 1957 to teach and coach five sports. The award was accepted posthumously by Academy Dean, Mick Maier on Wolfe's behalf.

I only went to Wayland for one year, but that year I went on to win the 1976 Wisconsin State Championship in doubles, my first year playing high school tennis. It was a big deal for a first-year player, and I was nominated for the same Wayland Athletic Hall of Fame as Coach Wolfe. I have not yet made it in though.

Mom came to watch me play in the State Doubles and she wore a shirt that said 'Rally Rolley'. Whenever the ball volleyed past her, she yelled, "Rally Rolley! Rally Rolley!"

Coach Wolfe would say, "Shut up lady, I'm the coach here!"

After winning that night, I got drunk and stayed that way for the next three weeks.

Coach Wolfe was tough on me. He often threatened me to light a fire under my ass, but I remained grateful for his leadership and for the positive influence he had not just on my tennis game but on my life.

In 1981, he received the Distinguished Service Citation, the highest honor Wayland Academy can bestow on an individual. The award recognizes outstanding service to Wayland. In 1997, Wayland Academy dedicated the Sol Wolfe Pool, a new 6-lane, 25-yard swimming pool to the Wayland boys and girls swimming teams and for student recreation.

When I was in college at Oshkosh, I went to visit him after hearing he had been confined to a nursing home. He had not changed much and was still as sharp in mind as he had always been.

"This place is miserable, Grant," he said. "No one in here ever played sports or is even interested in sports.

"Watch this," he said and reached over and grabbed a hotdog off the man's plate sitting next to him while he was praying. We were in the common dining room. "That son of a bitch doesn't even know I stole it," he said, popping the wiener into his mouth. "That's what I'm living with here, Grant."

He told me he loved me before I left. He passed away at age 79 in August 1995.

Coach Wolfe had more influence over me than my mother, father, or any of my future coaches.

After our campus tour, Mom and I unloaded the car. She came up to my dorm room to make my bed and make sure I had everything I needed. While she was doing that, I went to the bathroom. Just as I opened the door, the smell of weed hit me full in the face and there stood this dude smoking a doobie. He ducked out quickly and disappeared. I thought to myself, 'So much for preparing me for college!'.

After Mom drove off and I went to settle in, the dude was piled up on the other bed in my dorm room, having just fired up another joint. He held it out to me and sustaining his inhale croaked, "Wanna catch a buzz?"

He turned out to be my roommate, Mike 'Augie' Gerhardt, and we became fast friends. I had smoked some pot before Wayland and didn't think that kids at Wayland would smoke - man, I had that wrong. Ninety percent of the kids in my dorm smoked pot, and about 50 percent got stoned daily. I officially added smoking what were then illegal substances to my existing drinking problem. Augie was from just down the road from Madison and brought his car to Wayland, which we used regularly to leave campus.

Once again, I quickly made a lot of new friends. I made the basketball and football teams, but I got sick during football practice and was diagnosed with mononucleosis. It is a common virus among young adults and is sometimes called the kissing disease because infectious mono is spread through saliva passed by someone carrying it. The carrier may never have symptoms, but they can spread it. I wasn't doing a lot of kissing that I can recall, but I did a lot of sharing bongs and joints and probably beer glasses too.

I ran the gamut on symptoms. Sore throat, swollen glands, headaches, and fever. It took three weeks to recover from it causing me to miss the rest of the football season.

Augy's brother Mark Gerhardt, who we called Pork, graduated from Wayland the year before I did. He played tennis, so we hung out a lot even though he was finished with school. Pork told me about a popular pizza joint called Pasquale's Pizza where if you tipped the cook a little extra, he would send over extra pitchers of beer. It became one of my favorite hangout places to drink at Wayland.

Pork also informed me that all the tennis players smoked Newport cigarettes. I thought that was cool, despite Super Dave's warning, and lots of people smoked in those days - musicians, athletes, movie stars and the common man. So that's how I added cigarettes to my growing list of vices and bad decisions.

It was true. Wayland had a dress code, and the boys had to wear suits and ties, and the girls had to wear uniformed dresses to class every day. Most of my classmates came from wealthy families. I didn't, but as it turned out, there were a lot of kids there who came from more impoverished means than myself. One of the purposes of the uniform and formal dress was to build a sense of unity among kids from different financial backgrounds. It gave everyone a sense of identity, sort of like a school mascot, and it prevented the wealthy kids from standing out over the poorer kids by dressing in expensive designer clothing. It kept everyone equal, and it seemed to work because most of the student body I knew approved of it.

I guess this was part of the "good education" Mom wanted me to have, but don't get it twisted. By lunchtime every day, my classmates and I were getting high. Weed was a much more common sin at Wayland than it was at Lakeland. I doubt my mother ever knew that.

Wayland Academy had a smoking lounge in the dorm and students hid their bongs in the brick wall and hit them daily. There was a massive amount of pot available, practically out in the open at Wayland. The most popular conversation there was about who had the highest ACT scores, and I wanted to talk about sports, so it was not one of my favorite places to hang out until I met Terry Podgorski.

Nicknamed Ski, he was 6' 5", a good-looking, fast-talking dude who played football, basketball, and baseball. He was academically smart and streetwise smart. He and Augy kept a three-foot tall bong behind the shower curtain the entire 2nd semester and never got caught. Ski got me high on hashish for the first time right before biology class.

Later, a girl named Mary Maier who was studying to be a doctor, came up to me at the student union and asked me why I didn't talk to her in class today. She said she sat right next to me in biology. I told her honestly; I was stoned and didn't even notice her being there!

Ski got kicked out of Wayland in 1977 and went on to make it big on the Chicago Stock Exchange as an options trader. Today he is a boat captain doing boat tours on the Chicago River, and he has five kids. You just never know how some people will turn out. Yesterday's delinquents can become tomorrow's millionaires!

I enrolled at the University of Wisconsin-Oshkosh for one reason only: to play tennis on the collegiate level. I did not have any aspirations for a career in tennis, I just enjoyed the game and got a lot of encouragement from people who watched me play. Under Coach Wolfe, I had greatly improved my game, and I felt confident about my prospects.

Augy, my roommate from Wayland was again my roommate at Oshkosh my freshman year and we lived in a men's dormitory called Cleamans Hall. Unfortunately, I made things difficult for myself. I partied hard day and night for the first two weeks of my freshman year. I was plastered all the time, and I did not attend a single class. On the 10th day, I went down to the gym to play basketball and when I returned to my room at noon, there were seven guys sitting around hitting bongs. When they left to go eat lunch, I packed my stuff and took a bus back to Minocqua.

Even if I had made the tennis team, I would be ineligible to play so I decided college was not for me. My mother met me at the door as I walked into the house.

"What are you doing home?" She asked.

I said, "I don't like college."

"Then get a job," she said, and turned her back on me. Sometimes the silence can be worse than the lecturing and that is what I experienced from her. I don't know whether she realized how bad my drinking was or not, but I know she was not happy that I wasn't in school. She also knew it was a waste of time to argue with me and she could not force me to go. Obviously, I got a job working at a cranberry marsh.

The success of a cranberry harvest depends on the seasonal climate and the ability of the cranberry farmer to prevent frost from killing the fruit before it is harvested in the fall. This is a tedious process in Wisconsin because it starts getting cold much earlier in the fall than in Alabama, which is usually late October or November.

Cranberries are grown at a lower elevation than the landscape around it and in the fall that is 10 to 15 percent cooler than the higher elevation. The cranberry fields remain dry 90% of the year, but in the fall, the farmer irrigates the field with water to fill the bog and prevent the cranberries from freezing. They use a complicated sprinkler system to keep frost from collecting on the berries.

Workers harvest the cranberries by wearing rubber waders and wading out into the bog to adjust sprinkler heads and to churn the water using waterwheels to loosen the berries from their vines. Then the berries are corralled and pumped out of the bog and into a waiting truck.

Farming of any kind is hard labor. Unsurprisingly, I hated it. It had absolutely nothing to do with sports, or with my drinking problem for that matter. I was always late or didn't show up at all. I know that during this time of unrest with my mother, dear ReRe advised her to throw my ass out of the house.

I now know I could not make rational decisions about anything because I was besotted with alcohol, but I decided perhaps school *could* be bearable if I could play tennis. I worked at the marsh for only a couple of months and decided I could re-enroll at UW-Oshkosh in January, take some "crip" classes like most athletes do to pass academically, and still make the tennis season. It was either work in a bog or finding a way to get through classes so I could play tennis. I chose sports broadcasting as my major. What I did not count on was that I left campus the prior fall before tryouts and the 12-man Oshkosh tennis team was already in place. That would cause some headaches.

I think it's fair to say that most students have a fairly wild time in college; they drink and party a lot, and push the limitations of the educational system. I was not out of the ordinary in that regard, but the intensification I experienced personally was not in any way normal.

When I reenrolled in January, I didn't go back to the dorm but moved into a house at 136 High Street with two buddies Billy Werch and Ron Seymour. Ron was a pitcher for the UW-Oshkosh baseball team.

The football stadium end zone was across the street from our apartment house and there was a staircase with rail posts going up. Every time Ron won a game, he would knock down one of the rail posts. By the end of the year, there were only two left, and you had to be careful walking up the stairs. High Street was an appropriate name for what was going on there.

That was where I drank the mushroom-spiked Kool-Aid I mentioned earlier and pretended to be a windshield wiper; and where Lenny Lehnen and I dropped acid and started traipsing down the middle of the street with a stolen sofa. Earlier that night, Lenny and I dropped some acid and went to Oblio's Tavern and hit the cups. About an hour into it, I sat there flabbergasted as I watched a full bottle of vodka do high jumps over a bottle of rum.

"Holy shit, look at that, Len!" I said with fascination. "Wow!"

Every Tuesday night at the student union, they had a "Mingle and Tingle" happy hour with mixed drinks for fifty cents. Lenny found a doctor in Madison who wrote him a prescription for quaaludes, and we renamed it "Mumble and Stumble" because everyone was doing 'ludes' and drinking. I, myself, earned the nickname, Commander Quaalude.

We had keg parties almost every weekend and I never went to class. I couldn't be bothered with an education, but I had a college-sized big time. One of my favorite taverns was called Beaner's Bar. They had a shot and a beer for .50 cents and their motto was "You're not leaving until you're heaving." Five dollars went a long way in the 1970s.

So far, I had managed to avoid any significant run-in with the law but that was about to come to an end. A buddy of mine, Barry Lesieur and I were driving home to Minocqua one night from school when we stopped in Stevens Point, Wisconsin. We both got drunk and the next morning, hungover and hungry with no money, we skipped out of a Shoney's without paying the check.

We thought we had gotten away with it until a cop pulled us over a few miles past the restaurant. I got a ticket for driving with a suspended license.

Barry and I both went to court and the judge set the fine at $120 for defrauding an innkeeper.

"At least we got the food for free," Barry mumbled.

The judge looked up at me and said, "Mr. Rolley, that will be 10 days in the county jail," and crashed his gavel down on the dais.

I was astounded, "I didn't say anything!"

"That is a lie," said the judge.

I still don't know whether he really thought I said it, or he was just holding me responsible for the whole affair since I was driving, but either way, I spent 10 days in the

Oshkosh jail before getting out early based on the Huber Law Survey that grants inmates the privilege of gainful employment mixed with confinement during non-working hours. The law had been expanded to include absences for family emergencies, school and medical reasons. Oh, and by the way... Lenny is now a licensed drug and alcohol counselor, and Barry is a lawyer. Go figure that one.

I fell in love for the first time at UW-Oshkosh. Augy was dating a girl named Jill Peppler. She lived in the town of Oshkosh, and she invited me to join Augy at a party at her house. Early in the evening, they ran out of beer. Augy said there may be some in a cabinet downstairs, so I slipped down the stairs and was rambling around in the cabinets when I heard a soft feminine voice behind me.

"Excuse me, are you a burglar?"

I wasn't expecting anyone to be down there, so it took me by surprise, and I spun around to find a tall dark-haired girl with olive skin gazing back at me bewilderingly.

"N-no, just a beer drinker," I stammered. Damn she was good looking. "They are out upstairs, and I thought maybe...»

"You are a funny guy."

"And you are a beautiful girl," I had a talent for hiding my awkwardness behind humor and flirtation. "Why are you hiding down here by yourself?" I asked.

"I am Jill's sister, Julie. I'm still in high school so she made me stay down here."

Now that I had a good look at her, I realized she had a lean but athletic build and a gorgeous set of gams. She reminded me of a darker haired Raquel Welch from that movie One Million Years BC and I couldn't help but imagine her running around in an animal skin bikini, flexing those fast twitch calf muscles. She was able to completely distract me from beer and alcohol for a couple of hours.

Julie was 16 and a junior in high school. She ran track, which explained her strong curvy legs. I was immediately attracted to her but during the conversation that night, I discovered she had a boyfriend.

It was only a week later that I saw Jill and Augy out one night.

"Julie wants you to call her," Jill said handing me a piece of paper with her phone number.

I was intrigued. "I thought she had a boyfriend," I said hesitantly.

"Not anymore!"

I called her and set up a date. When I went over to pick her up, her father Manny Peppler shook my hand vigorously. "Would you like a cold one?"

He invited me in, and I met her mom, Marian. We had a beer together waiting for Julie to finish getting ready. I found them to be warm, friendly people. I admit at the time she was the love of my life. She may have been two years younger than me, but she really had her shit together and I did not. She had a job working at the local drug store, and I picked her up there often. We went out and had a lot of fun together, but she couldn't drink legally and wasn't really interested anyway. I behaved myself and didn't drink when I was with her, but she had to be home by 11 p.m. so I would drop her off and then go back out and drink until 3 a.m.

We dated for close to a year until she invited me to a family reunion. I guess it meant a lot to her, but I was not interested and told her I didn't want to go. She took it as an affront to her feelings. I said 'Whatever' and that was it.

I tried fervently to get her back, but she would have no part of it. She came by the house on High Street occasionally, and she was always cordial and inquired after me if I wasn't there. We stayed friends but I could never lure her back into a relationship. Last I heard, she still lives in Oshkosh and has grandchildren. I'm sure she is happy because she really did have it all together at a time when I was not there emotionally.

My sports broadcasting degree went in the same direction as my love life and classes at Oshkosh. Part of our class assignment for broadcasting class was teaming up with another student sportscaster in which one of us called an actual ballgame's play-by-play and the other acted as color commentator live on the college radio station WRST.

I teamed up with a classmate named Steve Reynolds to call a UW-Oshkosh Titans versus UW-Platteville Pioneer Pete's game. Everything went smoothly until the first commercial break. Both Steve and I were getting sloshed on the other side of the microphone and during what we thought was still a break, the listeners heard something like this:

"Hey man, give me another hit off that pipe." There was the clear sound of a pull off a bong and the croaking voice talking while holding the inhale for maximum effect, "'Ere man, we both need some good drugs to get through this suck-ass game."

"Anything left in that bottle of Yukon Jack?" You could hear clinking glasses.

"This team really sucks. This dickhead quarterback can't throw for shit."

"And our defensive line is a bunch of pussies."

On and on it went, until we realized we were live, but there wasn't much that could be done at that point.

For some reason they left us on the air for the rest of the game but come Monday morning, we were pulled off the program and kicked out of class.

Just as Super Dave is still my best friend, he remained a friend while I was in Oshkosh, and the summer before my sophomore year and Super Dave's junior year at Northland College in Ashland, we took a road trip to Naples, Florida.

The Meade family had a friend named Art Perkins who had moved from Minocqua to Naples, Fla. Dave said he would hire us to do some landscaping work over the summer. We loaded up the Datsun B210, stopped at Save More and bought $350 worth of beer and wine. The plan was not to drink until we got to Florida.

Fifteen minutes south of Minocqua, we popped the first "tin I love to touch", as our friend "Rooster" Wheeler used to call popping a tab on a beer can. We drank all the way to Sarasota which is a couple hours north of Naples.

We made a stop at the Sarasota Kennel Club where we won $180 in dog racing. We credited our win to the magical attributes of beer and decided to forego working, and instead, live as large as two broke college students could live.

We drove another couple of hours down to Sarasota and got trashed. We were supposed to start work with Art at 5 a.m. the next morning but instead, slept until 9 a.m. and headed back to Wisconsin. We decided I should go back to school and improve my college tennis game and Dave should go back to school and work on his college basketball game, rather than toiling away in Florida's hot sun.

The trip was not a complete waste though. We stopped at a Holiday Inn in Louisville, Kentucky where we got loaded and signed up to be Independent Beauty Consultants for Mary Kay Cosmetics at their convention at the hotel. We never made any money at it but we both looked pretty in pink!

Unfortunately, later that summer, I got my first of two tickets for Drinking Under the Influence. It was my first offense so I was facing two choices: I could go through a 28-day rehab and get my driver's license back in 60 days, or not go through rehab and lose my driver's license for a year.

I did not want to stay in Wisconsin all winter so as part of my plea agreement, so I got permission to serve it in Florida instead of Wisconsin, and I was assigned a day to report to Pinewood Drug and Alcohol Rehab in Ft. Lauderdale. I flew to Ft. Lauderdale, Fla. with $300 in my pocket. I started drinking on the plane.

I was so snockered by the time we landed I didn't realize we had a stopover in Tampa. I got off the plane thinking I was in Ft. Lauderdale and hailed a taxi for a ride to Ft. Lauderdale Beach.

"Don't you even know where you are, buddy?" the taxi driver asked. "You are in Tampa. It is a four-hour drive to Ft. Lauderdale from here."

I bought a 12-pack and hopped on a bus. I was no longer in school, so I didn't realize it was Spring Break. I had never seen so many people in my life and they were all set to party, so I fit right in.

I lost track of time and instead of checking into Pinewood the day I was supposed to, I went to the beach and rented a hotel room. There was a bar down the street, and I ran into a girl from Minocqua and proceeded to drink her under the table. Three days later, with forty-two cents to my name, I called Pinewood from a bar called the Elbo Room on Ft. Lauderdale Beach.

It seems my mom had already called them to make sure I made it and when the counselor told her 'No', she was frantic. They asked me where I was, and the rehab sent a car to pick me up.

"How far is to 'the place'? I asked the driver.

"Shut up," he said. "You have caused enough trouble."

Once I got settled into a room at Pinewood, I was sharing a room with a guy who wore a "Do Not Disturb" headband, so I kept my distance from him. When the doctor came in, he walked straight over to the window and stared out practically ignoring me, as if in deep thought.

After an elongated silence, he turned slowly towards me, put out his hand to take mine and said, "How is this working for you, pal?"

I didn't respond.

"You are going to get better," he said. It was impossible to tell whether he believed it himself.

A few days later, I was lying on my bed fully clothed staring up at the ceiling listening to the radio when a counselor named Tom Dugdale walked into my room.

"What are you doing with this freaking radio?" he demanded. It turned out radios and televisions were privileges you had to earn. I had earned nothing.

"I like to listen to baseball," I mumbled.

He held up a mutilated left hand with two fingers missing for me to see. "Got this in Philly from a guy sliding into second base. He was wearing steel cleats and sheared off these two fingers like he was slicing through sausages.

Should have seen the blood. It was like a massacre." He put his hand down and sat down in a chair across from me.

"You're making some progress and I'm a sports fan too, so I'm going to let you keep the radio."

"Nice of you," I muttered.

"Here are the rules going forward and you are not to break them, do you understand?"

I didn't say anything.

"You will get up at 4 a.m. and wash dishes at 5 a.m. You will clean your room and make your bed at 6 a.m. You will eat breakfast at 7 a.m. and then you have group therapy followed by individual therapy until noon. Do you understand?"

I snickered. "I get up at 11:30 a.m. I will see you at lunch," and I rolled over with my back to him.

"Let me explain this to you in the simplest of terms," he said. "I will drag your ass out of bed, as I said, at 4 a.m."

The next day, he did exactly that and he was not gentle about it.

I knew Mom was worried about me, so I sucked it up and called her.

"You are out of control, just like your father, Grant," she said. I could hear the concern in her voice, but she was not one for high emotion. "You must do better. You must remember who your father was and keep with rehab for as long as it takes. You do not want to end up like him, do you?"

For some reason, I felt like challenging her.

"Mom, you drink every night! Why don't you stop drinking? I'll bet you can't quit!"

"I don't need to quit, Grant." she said. "I have one drink after work occasionally and I drink a little bit socially. I don't need to stop because I don't abuse it."

Well, that put me in my place and honestly, it was the first time I realized she knew what was happening, but she had never confronted me with it.

I remember sitting in a chair, staring at a list of 12 Steps. By now everyone knows sitting around and studying material was not my strength. I said to Tom Dugdale, "This is insane. I'm a terrible student. I am leaving."

"No. You are not going anywhere," he said. "Your excessive drinking is what is insane. Your behavior when you drink is insane."

"How do you know! I never drank with you," I challenged him.

"You can't bullshit another drunk," he explained. Then he challenged me. "I'll bet you $20 you cannot do the full 28 days of rehab." He went to the door and opened it to leave. "But you will be back. Probably multiple times if you don't die first," he said and slammed the door behind him. He was partially right. I completed all 28 days of rehab.

Super Dave came to visit during a six-hour day pass and we played golf at Rolling Hills where the movie Caddyshack was filmed. Dave was working at a liquor store in Delray Beach, and he gave me a picture his Jim Beam sales representative gave him. It says, "Living well is the best revenge". It was the greatest gift I have ever received.

When I got out, I flew back home to Wisconsin for the summer. Super Dave picked me up at the airport.

"I have a drinking problem, Dave. I have to stop drinking."

He didn't mean to be dismissive of my problem, but he did not understand the difference in his ability to drink and control it, and my inability to drink and control it.

"Oh, Grant. You don't drink that much," he said. "Not any more than I do."

As I recall this conversation now, I can hear Charles' voice telling me, "Remember, a recovered alcoholic can enter the world of normal, but normal folks can't enter the world of alcoholism."

I had not yet met Charles at that time and Dave and I both were still young and did not understand the mechanics nor the seriousness of my drinking problem. He didn't realize any more than I did that I was an alcoholic.

I was required to attend AA in Minocqua when I got back from rehab in Florida as part of my requirements for getting my driver's license back in 90 days. Because I was well-known in Minocqua, I was afraid it would show weakness to admit to being an alcoholic, so for some reason, I decided to one-up everyone else.

"My name is Grant, and I am a heroin addict," I said in the first meeting.

A couple of days later my friend Rat Seiler held a softball party at his house. Our pitcher brought a half barrel of beer. I refused to drink but Rat started running his mouth about what a light weight I was. I was struggling mightily, and he made me so mad I shoved him through his fireplace, knocking the whole structure down.

"Remember, a recovered alcoholic can enter the world of normal, but normal folks can't enter the world of alcoholism."

Despite the struggles, I stayed sober for three months and during that drying-out time, I got a job teaching tennis. I have been teaching tennis ever since. I was in excellent physical condition, and we had won a doubles match with our biggest intramural rivalry. We were all meeting at the tavern for drinks to celebrate our win. I thought, 'What can it hurt to have a couple of beers with the guys? Oh, go ahead! You deserve it!'

Twelve beers later, I was officially off the wagon.

Grizz, also not understanding the seriousness of my affliction commented, "Twelve beers are not enough to screw you up, Grant."

It would be easy to place guilty blame on Grizz, but he wasn't saying it because he didn't care or was trying to enable my problem. He was like the rest of us. He did not understand alcoholism. We thought it was what everybody did. Remember, drinking is a common pastime in Wisconsin.

I succeeded in playing tennis three of the four years I was at UW-Oshkosh. During that time, I reached the third round of the Men's Open Singles at the Western Racket Club in Green Bay. I had to play the No. 1 seed, an Australian named Mark McMahon who played on the international tennis circuit. He crushed me.

"Okay, you beat me in tennis, but I will outdrink you at the bar," I boasted. I was up 15 beers to his 11 when he left.

Three years later after my first rehab, our paths would cross again, and it would be an important hookup. But tennis was a mixed bag of experiences at UW-Oshkosh under tennis Coach Jim Davies. When I got back to Oshkosh in January, I went to talk to him. While he was inducted into the UW-Oshkosh Hall of Fame in 2000 and was a coach there for 26 years, I was not as fond of him as the Hall of Fame recognitions reflect.

According to his Hall of Fame write-up, he was Wisconsin Intercollegiate Athletic Conference's All-Time Men's Tennis Coach who guided UW-Oshkosh to a 267-236 record with 10 conference titles. I might mention that means he lost almost as many matches as he won, but he received accolades too for coaching men's swimming and diving, and women's tennis. To me, he was just the opposite of Coach Wolfe at Wayland.

The team nicknamed him Dumbo, and despite the fact I was not exactly what you would call sober-minded, I considered him a class A asshole and the absolute worst coach I have ever seen in any sport to this day.

"Where were you this past fall?" he asked. "We had a freshman tournament, and I couldn't find you."

"I had to drop out and go to work," I responded with at least half a truth.

The team had a great schedule and played a lot of good teams. It would be competitive and challenging. I wanted to be on that team. I knew I was better than some of the guys chosen and while perhaps I did not deserve to make the team after leaving school so abruptly that past fall, the way I saw it, the team needed me, and he knew it.

"We already have 12 players," he said. "You can't play. There is no room on the team."

"Screw you! I am playing!" I yelled back at him.

I started just showing up for practice like I was on the team. I was no. 13 on a 12-man team, but I knew I could earn my way onto the team. Never mind the rules and Dumbo's rejection. Almost every night, I noticed two black guys smoking weed, drinking wine and sequentially volleying a tennis ball against a practice wall at the back of the courts.

The first practice was scheduled from 10 p.m. until midnight inside the gymnasium because there was snow on the ground. They put up four tennis nets and I was prepared to challenge the coach. When he saw me play, he would have to put me on the team. I shot baskets, waiting for a court, but Dumbo never showed up. I was pissed off, so I went to the tavern nearby and drank 15 beers.

The next night I showed up for practice and Dumbo was there, but he was determined to get rid of me. He gave me three tennis balls and said, "You're playing the No. 12 guy. If you win, you'll replace him." Before I knew it, I was down 9-0.

Dumbo started taunting me. "See ya, asshole!" he saluted before the match was over.

"Wait you, fat-ass," I yelled at him, then turned to my opponent. "You are not going to beat me because I'm better than you!"

That night, I came back to beat him 11-10. I was now No. 12 on the team.

The next day I went to Coach Davies. "Hey man, do me a favor. I want challenge matches until I lose so I can earn a better spot on the team."

He let me do it and I played and beat every player until I earned the No. 5 spot, which was pretty good as a freshman. There are usually six people playing challenge matches at a time, so I was in a good place. I had continued to see the two black guys volleying against the practice wall at the back of the courts, so I walked up to them one night and asked if they played tennis.

"No one can beat the wall," one of them said. He walked over and extended his hand, introducing himself as Jumping Joe Franklin.

"I have nicknamed you the "Walk-on"," he said. "I've been watching you and you are going to be pretty good."

A guy named Tom Cascarano moved up from the No. 2 spot to the No. 1 spot making him the team captain, but Dumbo wouldn't let any of the team members challenge him.

Tom liked me though and when he saw I was good, he too began calling me "Walk On" and requested I replace his doubles partner who broke his ankle halfway through the season.

Years later, he would be the tennis pro at the Mt. Brook Swim and Racket Club in Birmingham when I got a job at my current club, Musgrove in Jasper. When I saw it was him, I deliberately set up a lesson with him under a false name of Mark Seiler. When I went over to play him and he saw it was me, the look on his face was priceless.

I easily beat him and afterward assured him, "You are a bad tennis captain, but a hell of a nice guy!"

A few days after meeting Jumping Joe, I was driving downtown when I saw him walking that way.

"Hey man, hop in," I said opening the passenger side door.

"Thanks man, stop up here at that liquor store," he pointed.

I had never passed up a chance to buy liquor, so I pulled in. Jumping Joe gave me a liquor list: bottle of Easy Nights, bottle of Mellow Days, bottle of After Hours, and bottle of Steppin' Out, all made by T.J. Swan.

"We are going to drink four bottles of liquor." He said.

And so, we proceeded to do just that.

It turned out Jumping Joe was an All-Big 10 6' 4" center drafted by the Milwaukee Bucks. He injured his shoulder but still played eight seasons of pro basketball in Europe, drafted by the Dallas Cowboys and was the last cut for the 1972 Olympic team. I considered him a mentor and we remained friends until he passed away in 2022. R.I.P. my friend, Jumping Joe!

Back in my freshman year at the University of Oshkosh in 1977, our number one player was Bob Wolfman. Picture this: a 140-pound lefty who looked like Bob Dylan and lived like a stoner. Bob wasn't just great at tennis - he was also a killer foosball player, averaged 215 in bowling, and could hustle free beer at Kelly's Bar with his ski ball skills. He even taught me the ropes. Years later, at the same tournament where I met Joe Brandi, I ran into Bob again. We played, and I beat him 6-2, 6-2. The guy was an exceptional counter-puncher, taking down big-hitting college players left and right, so having him want to play number one doubles with me was huge. He even told our coach, Jim "Dumbo" Davies, to make it happen. I'm thankful for his support during that time. We've talked recently, and it's great to hear he's gone on to have a successful career in business.

During my second year at UW-Oshkosh, I met a guy named Joe Farley during a pickup basketball game. The guy was like a greyhound—fast, agile, and impossible to catch.

Afterward, we went out for beers, and I told him, "Joe, you might be one of the best athletes I've ever seen."

He laughed and said, "Don't tell anyone, but I'm only the third best in my family!"

Turns out, one of his brothers was drafted by multiple major league baseball teams, and another was the Wisconsin High School Player of the Year as a quarterback and safety. Joe told me about how Joe Paterno was in his living room one day and Tom Osborne the next. He ended up signing with Wisconsin but blew out his ankle, derailing his football career.

Joe played tennis too, and we ended up playing doubles together at UW-Oshkosh. He had this wild, almost Charles Manson look about him, and when we met our opponents, he'd launch into this crazy "You can't kill me— I'm already dead" speech. It rattled them every time. We still keep in touch to this day. Joe's got a son named Grant and a beautiful daughter working on her Ph.D.

Anyway, I flunked out my senior year, making me ineligible to play. Again, I went to Coach Davies and asked him to make an exception so I could play.

"Do you recall that trip to Las Vegas last year with the school band when you got drunk and passed out, making us late for a tournament?" He said.

"That's why I won't make any exceptions. Shit like that!"

I was a hothead, no doubt, and a drunk, but the entire team's beef with this coach was that he never established any hard and fast rules or guidance for the team. Yet when he got mad, he suddenly threw up non-existent rules to punish us. How could we follow rules that had not been established and now he was punishing me for breaking rules that didn't exist. I appealed to the athletic director, but he backed up Davies and said no.

At that point, I went back to the coach. "I am going to ask you one more time to let me back on the team!"

"I said no!" he bellowed.

I said some very foul things to him and yanked a tennis racket off the wall and smashed it onto the glass top table where he was seated. Pictures and glass flew everywhere. He grabbed the telephone, and I ripped the cord out of the wall, then got in my car and drove to Arizona.

CHAPTER 6:

MATCH POINT

I arrived in Tempe, Arizona in the dead of winter. What was I going to do in Arizona? I had no idea. I spent the next six months working for an apartment complex at Arizona State University and playing tennis every night with a guy I met from Switzerland. He and I played and won several tournaments and did a lot of drinking as well.

In the spring, I received a call from Super Dave. He was a counselor for a school in Eagle River, Wisconsin where he knew a kid named David Feldstein. David's dad was a multimillionaire from Beverly Hills, but they had a summer home with a tennis court in Eagle River.

The dad was taking private tennis lessons, but he told Dave he would like to hire me to instruct his entire family and business associates who came to visit. I went back home to Wisconsin and worked the whole summer for the Feldstein family making $100 a day – pretty good for a 19-year-old college dropout.

That winter on New Year's Day, I was coming home from a party. It was snowy and the roads were icy. I hit a patch of black ice and slid into a snowbank. My car was stuck, so I decided to just walk the rest of the way home. About 150 yards past my car, a familiar cop pulled up beside me.

"Grant, what are you doing?"

"I'm walking home," I replied.

He said, "I think you are drunk."

"I'm not going to say one way or the other about that," I replied.

He took me in for a breathalyzer test and I failed.

I went to my mom and told her all I needed was a good lawyer and I could get out of it because I was not behind the wheel of a car when the cop stopped me. Mom refused to get me a lawyer, so I got a second drunk driving ticket even though I was walking and not driving.

I returned to Ft. Lauderdale looking for a tennis job. I walked into the Hollywood Tennis Club and my old Australian buddy, Mark McMahon, was the head tennis pro there. It had been about three years since he beat my brains out in tennis at the Men's Open Singles in Green Bay.

"I beat *you* 15 to 11 in Green Bay, remember?" I razzed him, referring to my out-drinking him afterward.

He laughed. "What can I do for you, mate?"

"I need a job."

Mark sent me to the Bonaventure Racket Club in Weston, Fla. where I worked for the next three years, through good times and bad. I initially lived in a halfway house, but myself and an old man I met there, decided to rent a condo at Bonaventure. One day, he called 911 and claimed he was having a heart attack. He wasn't. He didn't have a car, and he just wanted a ride into town to get drunk. I never saw him again after that.

I had several fun experiences while working at Bonaventure. I played doubles in a Pro-Am tennis tournament with actor and lifelong tennis player, Lloyd Bridges. He was an elite athlete who for those who are old enough, may remember him for his role as Mike Nelson in the 1958 top ranked TV series *Sea Hunt*. He is also father to both actors Beau and Jeff Bridges.

He was a nice guy. I said, "I've seen all your movies."

"Really? Which ones did you like best?"

I had to admit I couldn't name one.

Ironically, my drinking ability often seemed to pay off.

One day, I was walking by the tennis courts while the great Australian player, Roy Emerson was giving a tennis clinic. He yelled at me, "Hey, Blue! Get me a few beers." Blue is a name for redheaded men in Australia. I brought back several beers, and we spent the next 15 minutes hitting sky lobs and seeing who could quaff the most beer before the ball came down. Later that day, I gave a lesson to FOX newsman Brit Hume.

Yep. Drinking could still be fun, but it was a cunning deceit and a powerful betrayal of truth.

I'm often asked how did I go to work hungover every day and keep my job? Didn't I have problems with bosses or customers? Nope!

I would wake up and go to work hungover, but whenever I started coming down and getting tired, the cocaine picked me back up. Before I knew it, it had become routine. I would come in from work, take a shower and go into town to have a couple of beers - only it was never two beers, it was 12 to 15. The next day when I needed a little pick-me-up, a couple of snorts and I was good to go!

It was not only a dangerous cycle but a vicious one as well, but I was still young. Once I started teaching, I could stay on the court all day. Maybe I sweated out the alcohol and some of the coke in the hot sun, I don't know, but I would be fine. Or thought I was.

I began hallucinating while I was still on the cocaine. It was especially bad when I tried to cut back or quit or if I went a couple days without it. I would come home and the first thing I would do is sneak in the front door quietly and make my way to the broom closet before they knew I was there. I would grab a broom and check the spare bedroom, look under the bed, even check the bathroom behind the toilet.

I just knew they were there waiting for me. I have always had a terror of king cobras, and these reared their wide hooded heads and peered at me through beady black soulless eyes, their forked tongues flicking in and out, shadowing my every movement to strike me right in the face.

One night, I laid down on my bed after checking everywhere else and realized, 'Holy shit, I forgot to check under my own bed.'

I had a fear of one unbeknownst to me, lying on the floor and silently rising and striking me while I was in bed, so I got up and looked under the bed and there they were. I saw a den of them, writhing in the darkness under my bed. I could see their green and black eyes staring out at me hissing.

I scrambled backwards on the floor like a child waking from a bogyman dream, trying to get away from them before realizing they were not actually there. I still remember praying desperately and promising God I would stop drinking and using drugs if He would just make them stop.

On another occasion, my boss Bob Sassano and I discussed incoming bad weather. There was a storm off the coast and based on which way it turned overnight, there was a possibility of heavy rain the next day. He said if it is raining in the morning, don't bother coming in.

I did a bunch of cocaine that day and when my alarm went off at 7 a.m. for me to get up and get ready to go to work, I heard rain battering my bedroom window. Oh, thank you, Lord I thought and rolled over and went back to sleep.

I woke up at 9 and the same thing, I heard rain battering the window, so I thought 'Beautiful!' and went back to sleep. When I woke up at 11 and heard rain hitting the window, I got up to fix myself a glass of orange juice. 'Wow, is it going to rain all day?' I thought, and I opened the curtains to discover there was a broken sprinkler head stuck blowing water like rain all over my windows.

"I cannot wait to hear your shitty story this time," Bob said when I went down to the office.

"You are not going to believe this," And I told him.

"You're right, I don't believe it," he said.

"But I can prove it!" I said, and he walked over to my apartment to see for himself.

I later went back to him and told him I was in trouble and needed professional help. He had been good to me and assured me he would work with me to get through it.

Fourth of July weekend, 1985, three years after my first 28-day rehab stint, I was in a dark place. I knew I was in trouble. Truth has a jagged edge that not only slices us open, but it rips and gouges chunks out of our soul. It is an ache and a reality that cannot be ignored. Even alcohol and drugs couldn't make it disappear because at some point, you must wake up from the stupor and there it is. Naked truth and bare-assed reality.

I was in excruciating pain. The kind of pain that brings strong, grown athletic men to their knees. I remember sobbing, tears streaming down my face as I drove home at 5 a.m. following a long day and night of drinking and snorting cocaine. I wondered if I had known my father better; been old enough for him to share his inner demons and talk to me about what his life as an alcoholic was really like – would he describe what I was feeling at that moment? Would his warning have deterred me from the path I had chosen?

Did he know that the *ankylosing spondylitis* was nothing compared to the damage the alcohol was doing to him? Surely yes! Wasn't the disease just an excuse to give up trying or had he in fact given up trying all those years ago when he left us with no money a year after I was born? Did he ever really try to rid himself of this proverbial monkey on his back?

I thought not, and for the first time in my life, I realized he was not the icon of fatherhood I had made him out to be. And being dead did not make him a martyr. All those years, I just wanted a daddy, a father, a mentor; but Wayne Rolley would never have been that to me. In fact, had I grown up with a father in the same condition I was in right now, how would *that* have affected me?

The father I dreamed of was a child's fantasy and a young man's folly. What if he did live with us and help raise us and was so drunk all the time, he stumbled and fell walking to midfield with me that memorable homecoming night? Perhaps my complaint would have been, 'Why am I stuck with *this* father?' Or perhaps I would rather have had *no* father, than one who embarrasses me like this?

I remembered how when I came back from spending those handful of days with him when I was 12, how I made a point of trying to find characteristics in myself that I could for the first time claim as my father's son. I remembered how proud I was of him and how I excused his and Doreen's drinking as a little odd, but not bad or dangerous.

Now when I looked in the rearview mirror, all I could see was him in me - a weak and broken man. Did I want to follow in his footsteps? At 23 years old, did I want to be a disappointment to my future wife and children, like my father was to us?

I had to accept my human frailty and seek help. Some people struggle for the strength to loosen the cruel grasp of drugs and alcohol, but many more lack the will to fight it. I had the will and the strength. I wanted to live life and live it well.

The second time I went into rehab, I packed some clothes and taped Tom Dugdale's business card to my dashboard. Tom had transferred from Pinewood in Davie to what was then called Ft. Lauderdale Hospital's Alcohol and Drug Rehab. I liked Tom, and I stayed in touch with him. I needed to talk to him - I wanted to talk to him. But even then, with tears streaming down my face and my life hanging by a thread, I couldn't summon the strength to walk into rehab on my own.

With Tom's information taped to the dashboard, I came up with a plan. If I got pulled over by the police - and considering the state I was in, it felt inevitable - I'd just tell them I was trying to find the rehab center.

For some reason, I headed for the beach and the next thing I remembered was waking up on a bench at the beach. I had lost a couple of days and my car. After that everything was a blur. The next time I woke up lucid was on July 8, handcuffed to a bed in the Ft. Lauderdale Hospital.

Apparently, I made my way to the rehab, but I have no idea how. It was after hours on a holiday weekend, so they were short staffed, and the door was locked. The nurses said I stumbled to the door and started banging on it, yelling at the top of my lungs, "I have a freaking appointment with Dugdale! Where is everybody? Let me in!" Then I smashed the glass.

When I came to, Tom Dugdale was standing over me. He spared me no mercy.

"You should be three years sober, but instead, water seeks its own level and buddy, you are in the sewer. What are you on?" he asked me, trying to assess what drugs and alcohol I had mixed.

"I don't really remember," I replied. "I think I took some Darvon or something."

"You dumb son of a bitch! You had passed the 90-day milestone and had more than three months of sobriety!"

"I understand," I replied.

"Well now, you have three choices to make. You can get locked up. You can get covered up - as in dead - or you can sober up. You had better choose wisely because if you choose wrongly, I promise you, you're going to damn die. You are not even going to outlive your drunken sot of a father!" July 8th, 1985, I said, "I'm done." And I was.

One day, a staff member told me, 'Grant, you have a visitor.' I went down to the lobby, and there stood Super Dave. With a grin, he said, 'Grant, let's go. I got you a six-hour pass - we're going golfing.' We headed to Rolling Hills in Davie, Florida, just ten minutes away, where they filmed Caddyshack.

That day became my first sober experience in this new chapter of my life. Dave had a couple of beers and kept singing, 'I got no use for your red apple juice!' He also managed to beat me out of $50 on the course. I'll never forget that day—it was a turning point, and Dave made sure it was unforgettable."

Soon after, I received a letter from Super Dave saying, "I met a girl and fell in love. How could I ever ask for more? She's rich as shit and her mom owns a liquor store!"

A wedding invitation followed, and I stood up at his wedding. He was also best man at mine 17 years ago. Dave and Stacy have been married 35 years and have two fantastic daughters and three grandkids.

Dave started a big basketball tournament billed as a last chance to raise money for Hurley Schools in Hurley, Wisconsin. Hurley is located just across the Wisconsin/Michigan state line from Ironwood where Dave played basketball at Gogebic Community College. Hurley has an excellent Girl's basketball program and Dave coached both his daughters Rebecca and Kat there in basketball. I love Dave. When he realized, like I did, what a serious problem I had, he was instrumental in helping me get sober. You can't put a dollar amount on love.

CHAPTER 7:
BACK IN THE GAME

The worst part was the withdrawals known as Delirium Tremens, also called Alcohol Withdrawal Delirium (AWD) and they come as quickly as 48 hours after withdrawal. They hit you unexpectedly in flashes, and there were a lot of them in the first 30 days of withdrawal. I would swear I saw something move. It would be enough to startle me before realizing it was nothing.

One day at work at Bonaventure when I had been clean and sober for several days, I was sitting at my desk when I could have sworn, I saw a shadow move across the wall at my feet. I was sure it was a snake, and I came out of the chair kicking at the wall and practically squealing in horror, trying to get it off me when Bob walked by my door.

"What in the hell are you doing, Grant?" he asked me puzzled.

My heart was pounding out of my chest, but I managed to make a joke out of it.

"I uhm, was working on my footwork," I laughed after realizing there was nothing there.

It's funny, people rarely noticed me high, but it was very clear I was sobered up because things got so intense with the withdrawals and recovery.

My first Alcoholics Anonymous meeting in Tampa, shortly after I got out of my second rehab was a lot different from the one in Minocqua when I defeated the purpose of rehab by lying about my problem. I was scared to death about it too.

I moved to Tampa after quitting my job at Bonaventure and wanted to start over. I have been sober and teaching tennis ever since then.

They start just like you have seen or heard in movies and books with, "My name is Grant, and I am an alcoholic."

"Hi, Grant. Do you have anything you want to share?" is the standard reply.

I explained how great it felt to be sober, how I had left my job teaching tennis, and how I had moved to Tampa to start a new, clean life. The more I shared with the AA group - about how I started drinking, my false belief that I could control it, and my failed attempts to moderate - the more I realized I wasn't alone.

Like all alcoholics, I was a distinction without a difference, but I wanted to be different. I did not want to be like this, like my father, an alcoholic who couldn't drink, but did anyway. I wanted so badly to be able to moderate but I knew I couldn't. I had to stop cold turkey as they say.

I listened and watched everyone else in the group intently. As I got a little more acclimated, I treated it like I had just been cut from a sports team and I was signing on as a free agent. I had to give it a try, otherwise I would never play at life again.

It takes a lot of bravery to stand up at a meeting and tell your own story. Afterwards, you feel a tremendous release. It makes you want to share it with others who are struggling because you know how liberating it can be.

I found out there were themes and ideas repeated daily throughout recovery and I have not found one to be untrue. Things like "Old-timers have much wisdom"; FEAR is False Events Appearing Real; HALT is Hungry, Angry, Lonely, and Tired; "A day at a time"; drunks are "dis-at-ease" making alcoholism a disease; "Keep it simple, stupid"; and seek "a higher power".

My personal favorite is the one I find to be the truest, "It works if you work".

I shared that my priority was getting a job. I was interested in either teaching tennis or transitioning into sports broadcasting. I even shared my drunken mishap at UW-Oshkosh.

One man pulled me aside and said, "If I can get sober, you can for sure get sober."

After the meeting, people held hands and said, 'Keep coming back.'

During my time in AA, I learned about the AA 12-Step set of spiritual principles for maintaining sobriety and how when practiced accordingly, they help break the obsession alcoholics have with drinking. I was introduced to the 12 Traditions that keep AA members unified and committed to helping each other overcome alcoholism the world over.

I discovered The Big Book, which is AA itself in book form with real stories about alcoholism and sobriety, what alcoholism is and is not, how you can beat it, as well as advice and support for spouses, family members and even employers since many alcoholics lose jobs or have criminal records for things like public drunkenness or traffic violations that show up on background checks when applying for work as a sober person.

I was given my first white AA sobriety token, the first of a series of small, round colored chips you earn when you meet certain sobriety milestones. They also act as a physical reminder to take sobriety one day at a time. You receive the white chip when you join AA or renew your commitment to sobriety. After the first 24 hours you get a silver chip.

In the past I had gone 100 days, so I was confident about the red, gold and green chips marking 30, 60 and 90 days sober. Ironically, 90 days is a watershed period and a danger zone where many alcoholics break down and either give up, or convince themselves they can drink and control it, like I did the first time after 100 days.

If you can get past that milestone, you work towards the purple chip marking four months, pink marking five months, and the dark blue chip marking six months of sobriety. Copper marks seven months and bronze marks one year.

After that, you get a medallion for every year sober, and we pray the AA Serenity Prayer based on Psalm 91 of the Christian Bible:

God grant me the serenity to accept the things I cannot change; the courage to change the things I can, and the wisdom to know the difference.

Biblically, Psalm 91 is known as the Psalm of Protection and the Soldier's Psalm. According to the Scott Psychological Centre, AA is the world's largest self help group, with meetings all over the world, and over a million members. It is a Christian-based program, one of the oldest self-help programs at 80 years of age, and the most successful.

All help while going through recovery is necessary in its own way but my sponsor whom I have mentioned repeatedly, Charles Edson, helped me get through some of the harder tasks. For instance, I was baptized at eight years old, but my family were not churchgoers and of course I was badly backslidden, although I never thought about what that meant.

If you had asked me whether I believe in God, I would have said of course. But when it came to relying on God's strength and not your own, when it came to praying to God for help, when it came to understanding grace and salvation - that requires a Higher Power, and I learned that power is real, and it exists!

Of course, now after going through a stroke and losing so many friends and family, I often wonder about Heaven and what happens there, as I am sure most people who believe in Heaven do. Will I see my mom and dad, old buddies, former pets?

Charles used to say whenever we parted company, "I'll see you at the top!"

"What is at the top?" I asked.

"Heaven sounds kind of good to me!"

Then he wished me good luck on my journey and told me to call if I needed him. He has since passed away, but he left a lingering impression on me! When you reach Steps 4 and 5, we are to make a searching and fearless moral inventory of ourselves and confess to God, to ourselves, and to another human being, the exact nature of our wrongs. Charles had me write these things out on paper and I confessed to him and God, everything I wrote down. I confessed to everything I could think of that left me feeling bad about myself.

One of the things that had haunted me for a long time was that I once told my mother, "When you get up in the morning and look out and see the birds chirping and right next to them you see me hanging from the same branch, just know it is your fault because you could not weather the storm with my dad!"

You say some stupid things when you are drinking, and I am sure that hurt her deeply.

"Are you sure you have confessed every single thing, no matter how bad it is?" Charles asked.

"Absolutely," I assured him. "I am not proud of any of them, and it has been hard to come to terms with it," I said, wondering why he was pressing me so hard considering the pain of my drunken confession.

He explained that he had an AA client in the past, an alcoholic farmer, who held some things back because he was too embarrassed to confess it. That pent up guilt did not free him from all his wrongs, and his guilt kept him bound to the alcohol.

"You must release all of it," he said, "or it won't work."

I saw where he was going with that, and I assured him I was not holding anything like *that* back.

"I just had to check. You can't shock a thoroughbred alcoholic, Grant," he said with a pat on my shoulder. He then burned my paper in his barbecue pit.

"There goes your old way of life," he said. "You don't drink anymore so there is no reason to ever go back there. Now all you have are living problems."

"What are living problems?" I asked.

"Broken air conditioners, tornado warnings, toothache, flat tires and things like that," he said.

I felt great joy at that moment, and it is the joy that is often the journey itself. Charles also got me to start reading the Book of Daily Prayer where I learned the importance of praying for the "gift" of sobriety. That is what it is for alcoholics – a gift, because otherwise I could not stop drinking without God's intervention. I still pray daily for it.

Another thing Charles did to help me was show me the tragic side of alcoholism. He pushed me to man an AA prevention hotline to get a feel for what other alcoholics and drug abusers are going through. It was very eye-opening. The first night I answered the hotline, the only thing the voice on the other end of the line said was, "I am going to shoot myself."

I was horrified. Suicide was not something I ever considered, and it made me feel panicked.

"Whoa, whoa, whoa buddy! Wait just a damn minute! Take it easy buddy and shut up. Don't say things like that!"

We started talking then and one of the things I asked him was what kind of bullets he planned to use. He didn't answer and I said, "Well, you need to know because you may shoot yourself and live through it and mess yourself up badly! You don't want to do that!"

By the time we hung up, I had talked him down off the proverbial ledge. I have often wondered what happened to him, I hope he is doing as well as I am. I know of a lot of alcoholics for whom it did not work out so well. Through the years, I have seen tragic ends come to heavy drinkers and alcoholics. The best athlete in my school at Lakeland was an alcoholic. If you'll recall what I said earlier, he stabbed himself and died.

Also, when I lived in Minocqua, I knew a young guy, 19 years old who left Bethels Bar one night walking home. He cut through a cemetery and fell into a snowbank where he froze to death.

A friend of mine, Tim Pukall, was found dead in a dumpster at age 45 in West Palm Beach. As they say in AA, but for the Grace of God, that could have been me. Another guy I knew got drunk and went deer hunting. He shot at what he thought was a deer but instead was a horse with a young female rider. The girl lived but she was lucky. Her horse not so much.

Thousands of people have been killed driving drunk or by a drunk driver. That was almost mine and Super Dave's fate but for the intervention from a guardian angel, we were spared. And I know people who got deeply and dangerously involved in drugs and drug trafficking. One of my tennis friends, Curt Johnson, worked for Tropicana Sunscreen. He had his pilot's license and was flying into Columbia to pick up cocaine and deliver it to Camp Lejeune when he got busted.

He spent nine years in prison. When he got out, he got sober and now talks daily to prisoners in prisons about the dangers of drugs and alcohol. Stories like these make me so grateful.

Something else I uncovered with AA is that it is okay to put aside your pride and be willing to ask for help when you need it. You can find help and a meeting anywhere in the world and that can be years after recovery. I found I had to do that at least once. Two years sober, I flew overseas to visit the French Open Tennis Tournament in Paris and after I landed, I called the American AA in Paris.

"The jet lag is rough, and I am thinking about drinking," I explained to the lady on the phone. "It isn't that I really want to drink, and I am not craving it, but I've been clean for a couple of years, and I am thinking about it. I just thought what the hell, I'm feeling like my body clock is screwed up and I don't know."

She assured me it was not uncommon.

"Jet lag is a frequent cause of people wanting to or feeling the need to drink," she explained. "It is okay." She invited me to a meeting the next day where she introduced me to a girl from San Diego. We spent some time going around the city together and everything was good after that.

Whatever it takes to stay sober, alcoholics must do it. By doing many sessions with a counselor and sponsor; following the 12 Steps and living by them and AA's Big Book; I am officially a recovered alcoholic of four decades.

I had spent most of my money on cocaine and for a while, I lived in a halfway house with two girls. They were into the heavy stuff, shooting up heroine. I was never tempted to do that, and I was on my way to recovery, so I had to get out of there although they loved having a guy to hang out with.

I put on my best salesman's pitch and approached an apartment manager named Paula Green with a mutually beneficial business proposition.

"What if I teach tennis here at the complex in exchange for rent?"

"Why would I do that?" she asked.

"Because there are a lot of apartment complexes around here and having a tennis instructor living on the premises is a perk for your tenants and a sales incentive for leasing," I told her.

She made a deal with me. "Okay. Get me 10 people who say they would be interested."

I came back with a list of 10 people on my softball team in Wisconsin.

"None of these people live here," she said puzzled.

"I asked them if they lived in an apartment complex that had a tennis instructor, would they take lessons and they said yes," I explained. "I asked them if they knew of an apartment complex that had a tennis instructor and courts, would they be more inclined to move there. They all said 'yes'. They can't all be lying."

"I don't know about you," she said quizzically.

She subsequently hired me to teach tennis in exchange for free rent and we started hanging out, then dating for a couple of years, which helped keep me occupied while I was going through recovery.

On the subject of money, during my party days I blew through a lot of cash - more than I care to admit. But when I got sober, I made a commitment to start saving and managing my money wisely. That's when I met Mike Wiginton of Capitol Management. I've mentioned Mike before, but it bears repeating: he's one of the sharpest and most knowledgeable financial minds I've ever encountered.

I pride myself on being able to out-argue most people, but not Wig. He has a way of cutting through the noise and getting straight to the heart of the matter. One lesson he drilled into me has stuck ever since: "It's harder to keep money than it is to make it." And, as usual, he's right.

Mike didn't just help me manage my finances; he reshaped how I think about money, discipline, and long-term success. It wasn't just advice—it was a wake-up call, and one I'm grateful for every day.

I met Joe Brandi playing in a men's tournament at the St. Petersburg Tennis Club in St. Pete. It was very hot, and so was I, throwing my racket and swearing a lot.

I heard someone say, "Dude, calm down and beat this guy. Then we will get a six-pack."

I settled down and won the match. He came up to me afterward and introduced himself to me. "I am Joe Brandi, tournament director and tennis pro here," he said.

Appreciative of the eye-opening scolding, I went to the store and bought the man a six pack. I explained that I quit drinking so I could not partake with him, and we immediately became friends. I thanked him for not defaulting on me for my temper, which he could have done.

"You just need to chill out. You are an okay player if we work on that temperament a little. Would you be interested in my helping you with your game?"

I was grateful for the offer. In turn for his giving me some lessons that significantly improved my game, I helped him work with some junior players at the club.

Joe has a daughter named Kristina who reached a career high of No. 21 in the world. He had coached her, and she had worked with the great Australian tennis coach, Harry Hopman. Joe's brother Andy Brandi was the University of Florida's women's tennis coach. Joe coached hard and worked me out very hard for about a month. He had some absolute 'no-nos'. Hitting the ball into the net was a felony that sent you to prison. As a pro or as an experienced player, you just don't do that!

Almost every day when we went to eat lunch, Joe would close his eyes and look to the heavens and say, "Life is like a light bulb, and you are going to shine bright."

Ironically, three years later, after I moved to Jasper, I was watching the U.S. Open on TV one weekend when I saw a roving reporter say, "I am here with Joe Brandi, coach to Pete Sampras."

Joe responded, "Life is like a light bulb and Pete's bulb is about to shine. He is going to win the Open and be No. 1 in the world."

Sampras did become No. 1 in the world. He retired after beating Andre Agassi in the 2002 U.S. Open. He won 14 major singles titles, a record at the time, as well as seven Wimbledon titles, two Australian Opens and five US Open titles in his career. That is the kind of coach and instructor Joe is and I have been blessed with his friendship and mentorship for 40 years.

That was where my life stood when I set up my appointment with Marshall at Paradise Lakes. After I got over my initial shock and accepted the job, I decided I could work at Paradise Lakes in the morning and for Joe in the afternoon. The following Monday I had lessons with six ladies, naked as the day they were born except for their little socks and shoes.

"Are you going to get nude?" one of them asked me.

"Not today," I demurred.

"At least take off your shirt," she said.

"Okay, I can do that," I agreed.

"We will eventually take you all the way," another lady said.

That night, I called Charles. "I got a job teaching tennis at a nudist colony can you believe that?" I asked.

"You are a recovering thoroughbred alcoholic being catapulted to a higher level of consciousness, Grant - so, no. It doesn't surprise me at all. Maybe you'll be promoted to archery!"

I had to constantly reassure Paula I was not messing around and that it was not a swinger's club. It was a clothing optional nudist resort. I invited Paula to come lay out by the pool in her bikini and she did.

"Look, it pays better than picking oranges and is a lot better for my self-esteem," I told her.

During the next lesson, one of the ladies asked me out on a date... I think.

"Will you be my date for Naughty Night?" she asked.

"What in the hell is naughty night?" I answered, intrigued.

"We all dress up in Victoria's Secret outfits. There is a band, and everyone gets drunk and slowly disrobes throughout the night," she explained as casually as if she was inviting me to a high school prom.

"No, I prefer not to be around drinking," I gracefully bowed out.

A fourth woman asked whether I was married.

"No, but I live with a lady," I said.

The setup was bizarre to me, but apparently it is not that uncommon. According to a very well-respected survey company called Ipsos, 14 percent of people identify as nudists and apparently in the 1970s, a New York Times article said American attitudes about public nudity had become more open.

If you are thinking being around them was a study in erections and affections, you would be wrong. Men and women, couples and singles just sat around the bar or at a table or in the common areas talking just like at any golf and racket club, only bare assed as a monkey and no one walked around with erections, hard nipples or even flirted. It was very "natural" and uninhibited. You did not see people making out or having sex – I guess that would be tacky? They did everything you would do at a resort only rather than wearing a bathing suit, they wore their birthday suits.

One lady explained it like this: She took out a tennis ball and held it up.

"Imagine this is a tomato," she explained. "One side is ripe, and the other side is rotten.

"If you were in a bar and there was a fat lady and a very fit lady, which one would you walk up to and start a conversation?"

"Probably both," I responded. I figured it was best to stay neutral.

For 10 minutes, she gave me a lowdown on nudist values, explaining that nudists judge people on inner beauty, and not their outer beauty.

"I am not judging anyone," I assured her. I didn't want to hurt anyone's feelings, and I had just made $60, so I decided it was a good deal.

After about six weeks, it was beginning to get to me. I was just not that comfortable with these exhibitionists, so I announced to the ladies I was leaving.

They said "Oh no! You can't leave now!"

They had the Nudist Tennis Championship of Florida coming up and they were playing against the Cypress Lodge Nudist Resort of Orlando! They wanted me to coach them to a win. Everyone arrived in Orlando on a charter bus fully dressed, but they quickly all disappeared into the locker rooms and emerged fully disrobed except for their socks and tennis shoes. We won the match 5-4.

On my last day there, I talked to a guy who always wore shorts rather than going totally nude when he played, and he was pretty good too. He said he was a cardiologist from Cincinnati, Ohio.

"Dude, tell me, what's the deal?"

"I don't know," he said. "My wife and I met this couple lying out on the beach in the Bahamas and we wound up having dinner with them.

They invited us here when we got back to Florida, and I've been coming ever since. Everybody's real chill. They just don't consider nudity to be a big deal."

I made a quick $1,500 and managed to remain always fully clothed. The money really helped me at the time. Paula and I eventually broke up. We grew apart as

I got more active in playing in tennis tournaments and joining the guys to go and watch tennis tournaments. Paula was never that big on tennis anyway. It worked out for the best because I was on my way to Musgrove Country Club in Jasper, Alabama where I would remain for the next 40 years.

No one will ever know how much I appreciate all the people who supported me during that transitional time, and there were many of them. There were also a lot of people who doubted me, and I thank them too. Many people fail and I had failed before, so I was not a good risk. That doubt, however, had the same effect on my psyche as I exerted on others teaching tennis over the years. It is what makes me a good tennis instructor.

I have a knack for figuring out what makes people tick, what buttons to push to get the best out of people. Everybody has buttons that when triggered, will boost them to a higher level than even they realize. Coach Wolfe at Wayland showed that to me. Once I find those triggers, I can teach people how to play and how to win at tennis. I especially like taking kids whose parents and other instructors doubt their talent and teach them how to really play – not just hit, but how to play the game.

It is not where you start – it is where you finish, and if I can find those triggers, and the kids have a passion for playing, within a couple of years they will be pretty good. That's how I succeeded in drug and alcohol recovery. I had to find those triggers in myself that helped me reach a higher level of accomplishment, more passion to live than desire to drink. I had to find a way to appreciate life's natural pleasures and not rely on manufactured pleasures with drugs and alcohol.

When I started going to AA meetings this time, when I looked at that list of AA's 12 Steps, I felt a power greater than myself at work. I knew it could and would restore my sanity, but I was no longer in some school environment where I had to pass a pop quiz. This was my life. I was literally fighting for my life and these 12 Steps had helped a lot of people overcome their demons.

"If you keep moving, depression can't catch you," Charles told me. "Depression is often what drives people to drink, and it can drive people back to drinking."

That had never been a problem for me, and I wasn't going to let it get a grip on me now. I stayed busy teaching and playing a lot of tennis. I quit going out to bars and wouldn't even go out to places where there was liquor at all. Don't misunderstand, things are not always easy, even free from alcohol, getting back on your feet can be tough. If not for some very special friends, I would not have made it through.

One of them is Juan Nunez. Juan was from Chile, and he was so poor as a kid, a guy gave him a tennis racket, but he couldn't afford to string it. He stuffed it with socks and learned to hit on a practice wall. He never had a tennis lesson in his life and was ranked in the top 140 in the world after turning pro. He coached Chris Evert and Gabriela Sabatina; as well as Arantxa Sanchez Vicario all the way to the French Open. He also had twin sons, Dylan and Tristian, both who were nationally ranked as junior players.

Juan is now in Delray Beach and has always had my back. He made some phone calls to help me get back on my feet after leaving rehab and after I left Bonaventure. Later that winter, Super Dave and I got tickets to the NFC playoff game at Lambeau Field.

When Brett Favre threw a touchdown pass to Antonio Freeman, he tossed the ball into the stands and Super Dave, and I came up with the ball. We were admiring it near the concession stand when a man we thought was a sports reporter from the *Washington Post* named David

Maraniss saw us and did an interview. The article was published in the *Post*.

We later found out he was an assistant editor at the *Post* who had written a book about Vince Lombardi called "When Pride Still Mattered". That was very cool and proof you can still have fun without drinking. Around that time, I won a tournament in Tampa that marked a big moment for me and my tennis game. The guy I beat in the finals asked where I was from. I smiled and said, "Ft. Lauderdale rehab. It was due to the gift of sobriety!"

In Tampa, I played a small part in Mark Keil reaching a no. 32 ranking in the world in doubles. Mark was from Albuquerque, New Mexico, which is not a place known for tennis. He is proof that how good you become is a matter of talent and willingness to learn and not where you are from. He was playing for the University of South Florida when he broke his foot. He walked into Avila Golf and Country Club in Tampa where I was teaching, and I recognized him.

"Hey pal, just because you broke your ankle doesn't mean you can't learn to volley with Grant Rolley," I teased.

We became friends and he agreed to take some lessons. Shortly thereafter he went on tour and made $1.3 million playing professionally. In 1992, he beat Pete Sampras, one of the game's greatest players at the time. I asked him how he did it and he said he played out of his mind. He had a strong belief system and believed he could play with the best.

During that same time, I attended the United States Tennis Association Men's 35's National Clay Courts Championship in Tampa where I met USTA professional Juan Díaz. Diaz was raised in Cuba but moved to Tampa in 1969 where he played on the varsity team at the University of Florida. In 1975, he was Southeastern Conference

Champion finishing No. 1 in the singles division and went on to become a three-time All-SEC.

When I met him, he was the tennis teaching pro at Palma Ceia Golf & Country in Tampa. Like Joe Brandi, he helped me a lot with my own game. When I was offered a job with Musgrove Country Club in Jasper in 1988, Juan encouraged me to look up Charlie Owens, by far, in my opinion, is Alabama's best singles tennis player.

My current favorite tennis professional is Nick Kyrgios. Sure, he's known for breaking a racket or two, but that's nothing compared to the scandals we've seen with doping. Nick's not just a great tennis player—he could probably beat every ATP player in basketball too. He's a straight shooter, a genuinely cool guy, and someone who gives back. I know for a fact that in Australia, he's bought groceries for families in need. That's the kind of person I admire. One thing on my bucket list is to hit tennis balls with Nick, and if I ever win the lottery, I'm taking ten friends to the World Series of Poker—because sober lives matter!

People often ask me, 'Who is the GOAT in tennis?' My answer is always John McEnroe. This usually raises eyebrows, and people are quick to disagree. But let's not forget—John McEnroe is the greatest doubles player in tennis history. And last time I checked, doubles is very much a part of tennis. Federer, Djokovic, and Nadal may have been superior in singles, but they hardly played doubles at all.

That advice led to a long-term friendship. Just before getting the job at Musgrove, I gave a lesson at Avila to a guy who offered me a job with Home America Realty. It consisted of 12 apartment complexes, and I got free rent and a little compensation to teach at all 12 complexes which is where I was before coming to Musgrove.

I often say now it wasn't that hard. There are other alcoholics who would say quitting drinking was the hardest thing they have ever done. Even more of them will say they have to fight that monkey on their back every single day, even after 30 or 40 years. It wasn't like that for me because I found my boundaries and my buttons. I absolutely knew I had to quit, and I was willing to do the things on that 12 Step list.

I am still not a finished product, but like everyone else living on this little planet, I am always trying to improve. I found that once I submitted to Him, the joy of God has always been there and never leaves me when I call on Him, even today.

CHAPTER 8:

IN THE SWING OF SOBRIETY

I was three years sober when I moved to Jasper to take the job at the Musgrove Country Club. I have been there for the past 35 years. I never looked back, although I have relived a lot of it in sharing this book. I've said before, I seem to attract real characters when it comes to friends, and it didn't take long after coming to Alabama to meet a new one in Jerry Gardner.

During the Musgrove job interview, Jerry sat next to me, silent during most of it, wearing a cowboy hat and smoking a cigar. As things were winding down, I turned to him and said, "You must have some questions for me?"

He did, but I misunderstood the question. I thought he asked me, "Are you winning any?"

"Yes, sir, every day!" I responded.

There was an odd round of laughter. He stood up to leave, tipped his hat, and said, "Hire that fella," and walked out.

On my first day of work, he told me I misunderstood his real question, but my answer was priceless. I was a little confused. "What question was that?"

"I asked you if you were 'getting any'," he said, and we both had a big laugh. We became great friends after that. Jerry was inducted into the 1995 Alabama Tennis Hall of

Fame and passed away in 2012. It was a blessing to know him.

When you move somewhere new, it is always good to know people in high places, or if you are an alcoholic, people who can get you out of low places. We just recently, only a few days before I finished this book, lost a great friend in Haig Wright. Haig was an independent insurance representative at Byars/Wright Insurance in Jasper. The thing that most stood out about him was his sincere and boisterous laugh when he stood up and shook my hand.

I had just been hired at Musgrove and although I was three years sober, I still had the DUIs on my driving record, making it difficult to get affordable car insurance.

"I used to drink a lot, Haig, but I quit three years ago, and I no longer touch the stuff." It felt good to say it and mean it. And if you live in a no-fault state where not having car insurance is illegal, you know what a big deal it was for him to make it happen for me. Another blessing.

Haig was more than just my insurance agent he was a great doubles partner in tennis too. He and I played in many tennis tournaments over the years and won most of them, including three Alabama state titles in the 25's, 30's, and 35's age divisions. I coached all four of Haig and his wife Robin's kids in high school too, including Haig Jr., Oliver, Amy, and Molly.

True to Juan Diaz's advice, Charlie Owens was one of the first people I sought out when I got here. Charlie and I became friends while he was teaching at the North River Yacht Club in Tuscaloosa – home to the University of Alabama.

Originally from Tuscaloosa, Charlie played at the University of Florida before flunking out and transferring to Samford University in Birmingham. He beat a lot of great players including Arthur Ashe, Roscoe Tanner and Vitas Gerulaitis in his professional career.

One of the first tournaments we played in was an exhibition tournament at Musgrove here in Jasper. He had already retired from the professional circuit, but I offered $250 to play with him.

"For $250, I'll have to kick your ass," he laughed.

There was no practice or warm-ups. He assumed any challenger had a good serve and if I happened to give him a shoeshine, that is, hit him in the feet in front of everyone, showing how badly I sucked would be punishment enough.

I was never intimidated playing against any of the famous or professional players. In fact, I played my best when I played Charlie in that exhibition. I must admit though, when the tournament emcee introduced us, my inner consciousness heard a distorted version of it: "The player on your left is Charlie Owens, ranked no. 35 in the world in singles, winner of the Orange Bowl International Tennis Championships, and he was the 1972 NCAA Division II Champion at Samford University.

"On your right is Grant Rolley from Minocqua, Wisconsin who has never done anything."

I won five games, so I was no slouch, but he beat me 7-5 and it was the best match I've ever played with so many people watching. Charlie is a one-of-a-kind guy, a country boy at heart. There are a lot of stories about him. For instance, while on the circuit, he would show up at tournaments with a sleeping bag and camp out on a porch or in his car because he didn't like traveling and staying in hotel rooms.

We played doubles in some national tournaments. On the court, he was what I would call a showman with grit because he is so competitive. Playing with him has been one of the highlights of my career.

While I'm talking about Charlie, I've got to mention something unforgettable - he was in the movie *Stand By Me*. His famous line, "Let's go, Lardass!" during the pie-eating contest, is one of those moments that sticks with you. It's a small part, sure, but it's part of a classic film, and that's pretty damn cool if you ask me.

My friend Bob Stock is an example of natural talent and determination. Now in his 80s, he taught himself the game and earned a scholarship to UCLA, later transferring to the University of Tennessee. He played on the USTA tour for 60 years, but back in the early days of his career, tennis pros didn't make much money even when they won. He had to live out of his car when he traveled to tournaments, and he got stranded while playing in Europe and had to win a tournament to make enough money to get back to the U.S.

He went on to qualify for Wimbledon and had a great career. Today, Bob is in the Top 5 in the world in the 80s age division. He lives in Hanceville and he and I still practice together a great deal. We also talk about spiritual things and his wisdom has helped me a lot. I guess I was most star struck meeting one of my favorite players, John McEnroe when he played at the Birmingham Jefferson Civic Center on the Seniors Tour.

My buddy Steve Susce, a ticket broker with AAA Tix in Birmingham got me a pass. Honestly what Steve does is like trading on the stock market. He gets me tickets to anything I want to see including the Super Bowl, Final Four, the Masters, and every college game in any sport, in any city. I have never been so grateful to Steve as when I walked by and saw a guy feeding McEnroe tennis balls.

McEnroe said, "Hey, come on and give me some more."

I stepped in and started feeding him balls and he volleyed them back.

Afterwards, when I went up to shake his hand, he commented, "Dude, you got great hands."

I said, "I know Johnny Mac, I've rolled a lot of joints in my life."

He gave me a high-five and we took a picture. He has a big personality, and my friends say we have a similar temperament. Maybe that's true. I broke a few rackets in my day, I mean everyone who plays sports has their moments, but I never thought I had an anger management problem.

I joined Walker High School as a tennis coach shortly after coming to Jasper. The school later changed its name to Jasper High School, and I got very busy teaching at Musgrove Country Club, so I left for a while. But during my tenure there as both the official and non-official tennis coach, I instructed a lot of excellent players.

In Jasper, I had the privilege of coaching some truly talented players. Shannon Johnson stood out as the No. 1 player on the Jasper team during my first year coaching at Walker. Alongside Shannon were William Johnson, Cole Johnson, Jud Allen, Mary Beth Murphy, Callie Bell, Bebo Dutton, Janni Westerman, Greyson Barber, Scout Barber, Alex Barber, Olivia Hayes, Clay McCoy, Jay McCoy, David Donaldson, Atticus Brown, Anna Donaldson, Erin Mosely, Kristin Mosely, Mike Wiginton, Andrew Wigington, Ben Hicks, Haig Wright, Oliver Wright, and Reed Pilling. Each of them brought their own unique talent and dedication to the court, leaving a lasting impression on me and the program.

I'm not saying you don't run in tennis, but really, you do not have to run as much as you think. One of the things

I teach all my students is to look at the tennis court as a big game of tic-tac-toe. If the ball is here now, where is the next place it is likely to be? Over there. That is what I meant earlier when I was trying to convince a doubtful Coach Wolfe at Wayland to take a chance on my natural athleticism. Most athletes naturally anticipate the opponent's next move and are ready for it.

The problem with new tennis players is they wait to run in reaction to the next volley. I teach students to anticipate where the ball will land when it is in the air. That way you are already there when the ball gets to you, and it becomes instinctive. I got that ability from playing other sports. When you learn to dribble in basketball, you must be ready to burst. Most basketball players make good tennis players because in basketball you are constantly moving your feet.

Think of it like getting ready and set for a footrace. You don't stand around erect and when the gun goes off, get set. You start from a momentum stance, ready to burst when the gun goes off.

One day, this kid came strutting by the tennis court. There was something about him, so I suddenly tossed him a tennis ball. He snagged it out of the air left-handed, then said to me, "Is that all you got?"

I was immediately impressed with this kid, so I asked him whether he played baseball.

"Yeah. I'm pretty damn good too," he said.

"Really? Well, in baseball, you only get up to bat every what? Thirty minutes?" I asked him. "I can tell you are a ladies' man."

That 7th grader looked me straight in the eye and said "Dude, you won't believe how much I get."

"Well, in baseball, you sit most of time in the dugout where the chicks can't see you," I said. "In tennis, when you play, and especially in tournaments, you might be exposed to hundreds of babes watching you play."

"Yeah? I'm starting to like tennis a little more," he said.

"You'd be very good at it."

"You're just blowing smoke up my ass," he accused me.

"Listen, tennis is all about footwork and you're a natural mover. Anybody can learn to hit, but you are way ahead in your natural ability to move."

That kid was Ben Hicks, and I got him to start playing tennis in the 8th grade, which is late for most kids. He got a scholarship to Wallace-Hanceville and won three State Championships as a junior.

It takes a little divine justice to get back some of what I dished out to my coaches. As a high school coach, I take great joy in knowing that Joe Brandi nor Coach Wolfe ever went easy on me and they not only positively affected my game, but they improved my attitude too. A lot of instructors and coaches in dealing with kids don't understand that you must be honest. You must make kids understand that some talent is inherent but much of it can be taught. The rest can be earned through hard work and passion.

There was a kid I read about from Minnesota who had several coaches who constantly told him how good he was, that he would make millions playing professionally as if he did not need improvement. He went to North Carolina State as a walk-on and was quickly cut from the tennis team during tryouts. He went back to his dorm room and hung himself.

It is a sad story, but you must challenge any athlete and regardless of their talent, make them understand competition is brutal and anyone can be beaten on any given day. I was tested by a "Little Me" on my first day as head tennis coach at Walker. I instructed the whole team on day one to warm up by running two miles.

A kid named Dwayne Wiginton challenged me.

"I ain't running two stinking miles for a damn Yankee!" he said and earned significant laughter from the team for his audacity.

"The North won the war. What happened there, big boy?" I replied. "You don't run. You don't play." I retorted.

"I was number three on the team last year. You need me," he scoffed.

Sound a little familiar?

"I don't live in the past. I'm only interested in the present and the future," I answered. "All you've got is a haircut and a forehand, so I'm sure I can find some Stoner to take your place."

"You don't know how good I am!" he yelled.

"I've seen enough."

"How about I kick your ass, put you in the back of my truck in a garbage can, and deposit you on Highway 78 while I enjoy a shake at McDonald's, watching you get hit by semi-trucks?"

You have to give the kid points for originality!

"Get lost," I said, knowing I was about to 'get the bull' for my unyielding stance.

Sure enough, the next day, Bull Wiginton, Dwight's hard-nosed, tough guy dad walks up to me before practice. "Are you the new tennis coach, and did you tell my son if he didn't run two miles, he could take his happy ass to the house?" he asked.

"Yes sir, absolutely," I replied.

"Thank God somebody stood up to his punk ass," he said to me, then yelled, "Dwayne! Give us four miles, right now!"

Dwight threw up his arms in defeat and started jogging.

"Put it there," Bull replied putting out his hand to shake.

Dwayne was the best trash talker I ever coached. He even outdid me. Walker went on to have a great season and finished second in the State Class 6A by two points. Our No. 5 player had to default due to a detached retina, but I believe had he played, we would have won.

As I said, I got very busy with teaching at Musgrove, and I decided to leave coaching high school. I was never crazy about the administrative aspects of any school as you can imagine, and I didn't have to deal with that at Musgrove.

A few years ago, Jay Todd, who is currently on the staff at Gulf Shores High School, but was Jasper High's defensive football coach at the time, approached me for help. He is a good friend, a big Green Bay Packers fan, and we often go to Packer games together.

He is the best defensive coach the school ever had. They won the state championship, but he had not only never coached tennis, but he also didn't play tennis.

"Listen, the school just made me the tennis coach and I don't know shit about tennis!" he said.

I was fine with helping him and the basketball coach out, although I am not paid nor am I an official school coach. I do go to most of their matches and do whatever is needed to help them win. One year, we had four freshmen on the tennis team, and I felt strongly that we had the talent and ability to win a title, but I was concerned the young team itself didn't have the confidence they could win.

I had a buddy, John Mack who owned a private plane. All I needed was something that would give the young team a two-point edge and I felt they could win. John said all he wanted from it was to shuck some fresh oysters at his favorite Mobile oyster bar.

I had approval from the students and their parents, as well as the athletic director, who all thought it was a great idea. John's pilot picked up the team at the Jasper Airstrip and flew us the 35 minutes to Mobile where the tournament was held.

When we got there, John pulled out a Centurion card and bought the entire team lunch. Great to have a friend like that! What followed was the most dramatic high school tennis match I have ever experienced. As a freshman, Oliver Wright won the No. 2 singles position on the Walker team. He and Reed Pilling made the finals and ranked No. 1 in doubles against U.M.S. Wright Preparatory in Mobile. They were one point away from the team title when things got tense.

Oliver hit a ball on his court and a guy from U.M.S. Wright yelled, "Hey! That ball was out!"

Oliver yelled back, "I'm playing No. 1 and you're playing No. 3, so shut the hell up!"

Now tempers had flared, and they kept going back and forth at each other. After about 20 minutes it came to a head when a kid from the prep school deliberately hit a ball at Oliver, and Oliver shoved the guy in the chest.

The prep school's entourage stood up and started yelling, "You bunch of damn rednecks!"

A Walker team father stood up and said, "Who are you calling a redneck, boy?"

The judges defaulted on Walker because of Oliver's shove.

"I'm sorry," Oliver said to me.

"Don't worry about it," I answered. "Next time, punch him in the mouth!"

In the meantime, there was an error in the team scoring, so despite the default, it still came down to us or them. We wound up winning the match by one point.

Walker fans stormed the court. It was the greatest win of my career. I could not have been prouder of those kids, despite the default.

Oliver and Reed are still among the most memorable of all the kids I coached and that fall, we won the title. True to form, in September, the school superintendent called me down to the office.

"Rolley, I could have lost my job for that little stunt you pulled last spring flying the men's tennis team to Mobile."

"Why? I'm not a pilot. I didn't fly the plane. And I had parental approval and the athletic director's approval," I argued. "Besides, in case you have forgotten, last spring, the girls team drove down there, they all got drunk and went to a Widespread Panic concert, and they didn't even win the damn match."

Jay backed me up and the guy was left sitting there with his mouth open.

"Obviously there's a communication problem!" I felt defiant because in all the years I worked for them, they never said thank you; I was now doing it for no money, which is fine, but they should know what they are talking about when they file complaints.

The following year, John flew me and 10 other guys on his private plane to Mobile for the tournament and Walker won again. This time, I rented a limousine to drive us home to Jasper where the mayor met us and congratulated the team. I owned some stock in the Packers franchise, and I gave it to Jay for supporting me in that dispute.

Tennis has given me a front-row seat to some unforgettable moments—some intense, some hilarious, and others deeply meaningful.

At a men's 55 singles tournament in New Orleans, I was playing on the court next to a match that took a sudden and violent turn. One guy landed a single punch, knocking his opponent out cold. In my opinion, it was just two guys getting after it—end of story.

But the funniest story comes from a tournament in Huntsville, Alabama, where I played a guy named Jody Brenner. Every time Jody won a point, his dog—stationed just outside the court—would bark on command. Every single time. Finally, I told Jody, "Man, shut that dog up!" Without missing a beat, he looked me dead in the eye and said, "I can command him to attack you."

We ended up playing six times, and I managed to win every match. But despite the competitive fire, we became great friends. Later, Jody was diagnosed with leukemia - a battle he faced with the same tenacity he brought to the court.

In 1996, I actually took Jody to the Super Bowl in New Orleans. We played in a square game during the first quarter and walked away with $2,000. It was one of those rare and perfect moments where everything felt right.

Jody is one of the smartest guys I've ever met, and I'm happy to say he's doing well today. Our friendship is a reminder that tennis isn't just about the matches you win or lose—it's about the people you meet along the way and the stories you carry with you.

We have a lot of great players, and I have developed a lot of great friends at Musgrove over the years. I received an announcement in the mail for a national father and son tennis tournament in Sarasota, sponsored by the USTA. I called the tournament organizer to ask whether it had to be a biological father and son. The guy rudely hung up on me. It was not a stupid question, there are a lot of legitimate fathers and sons who are not biological.

My buddy Joe "Boogie" (pronounced 'boo-gee') Franklin was a member at Musgrove and a very successful car salesman in town. He was 60 years old and clearly old enough to be my father, and neither of us had any kids at the time.

I acquired a fake ID for him and changed his name to Joe Rolley, but the USTA didn't check IDs, or at least they didn't that year. All we had to do was sign up. He was worried we were going to get caught but even if we had, they wouldn't do anything but kick us out of the tournament. By then we would have at least had some fun.

For anyone who questions the fairness of it, we lost the first two matches, so we were out of the competition, not taking anything from anyone but lasting memories. Afterward, we caught up with a team from California. The father explained he was on the tour circuit but realized he did not like the grind, so he gave it up and became a lawyer. His son commented that Boogie and I talked a lot differently. Boogie was bred southern. I was a midwestern transplant.

"Well, you see son, it's like this," Boogie explained to the kid. "His mama ran off with some boy from Milwaukee where Grant grew up. We hook up once a year and take trips together. Last year it was bass fishing; this year it is tennis."

Boogie is still around at age 82, still selling cars. I call him my "Musgrove Dad" and he is the closest thing to a father I have. Roger Hill is another good friend, a good old country boy and family man born and raised in Jasper. He fought in Vietnam, so he is as tough as they come. He was also a successful businessman and coached baseball. Roger and I played together in the Jeffco tennis tournament in Birmingham and came in second. I have had my share of tennis highlights and prestigious wins over some fantastic players.

Dan Lucas and I met at River Chase Country Club in Hoover, a suburb of Birmingham. He was the tennis pro there and I played him three times at tournaments and lost every match. I was bothered that I couldn't beat him, so I sat down and watched him play. I noticed he rarely missed the ball. I invited him to play doubles, and it turned out to be a very instructive match. Together we have won six state titles in various age divisions. He has a very high tennis IQ and helps me grow as a tennis pro. He also introduced me to the Alabama Hall of Fame.

I took a set from the tennis pro at Anniston Country Club. Peter Doohan was top 20 in doubles and beat Boris Becker at Wimbledon. He had a career high of 41 in singles. Dan and I lost to Peter in three sets, twice at the Mt. Brook Club tournament. The frustrating part is, Dan and I were up 4-1 in the third set.

Dan said, "We can raise our lesson prices by $2 after we win this match!"

Unfortunately, we lost.

I beat Mark Harner who was once ranked No. 543 in the world; had a win over Calvert Bibb who won a gold ball in Men's 25 singles; and won against Jimmy Weinacker, winner of eight gold balls in national father and son championships with his son Jay. In singles, Jimmy and I split sets. During the 10-minute break, I took a shower and smoked a cigarette. He reminds me of that all the time.

People say tennis is the sport of a lifetime and I agree. I am now in the 65's division but there are 70's, 75's, 80's, 85's, and 90's age divisions. Yes, people still compete in tennis up into their 90s. Dan has a theory that those who continue to play well up into older age have good genes and have avoided serious injuries throughout their lives, so they can still move lithely. They also have developed wisdom concerning the game.

Coach Wolfe, my tennis coach at Wayland Academy told me years ago I was naturally good at head games against my opponents, so I have always done a lot of trash talking. When but when I got nominated for the Alabama Tennis Hall of Fame, my refusal to "be nicer" and back off the mind games was my downfall.

I don't play to win friends and influence people, unlike some. I just play to win. As I said earlier, the first time Dan nominated me, I did not get in. The next year however, 2018, I was nominated again and a guy on the committee told the panel he had played me six times and I kicked his ass every time.

"He's really a good guy, just very competitive," he told them. "If you look at the list of people who are in the Hall of Fame, a lot of them have broken tennis rackets. That's part of being highly competitive."

I got in unanimously that year.

Look, here is the truth. I'm not everyone's favorite beer flavor on the tennis court, and I understand and accept that; but I try to make up for it by paying forward the goodness that has been shown me by others at different times in my life, and the mercy God has extended to me. I give more free lessons, especially to kids, than any tennis professional I know. I enjoy helping kids because if I could have taken lessons when I was a kid, I could have been a lot better a lot sooner than I am now.

I also have positive messages coming from my alcoholism. I currently have a student in his third marriage. After sharing with me his drinking habits and actions following it, he asked me if he is an alcoholic. I told him he might well be. "You need to stop drinking and if you cannot stop, then call me and I can help you." And I feel that way about anyone with a potential or existing problem with drinking alcohol. I refuse to let people stay in that terrible place if I can help it.

CHAPTER 9:

WINNING SET

I was 47 years old when I got married. Super Dave stood up for me at the wedding and reminded me, "Don't screw it up, Grant!" "I got this!" I assured him.

We've always had a lot of fun as a family. I once took a trip to Minocqua and went fishing with Super Dave. In 2002, I had been clean and sober for over 20 years when suddenly, I began having headaches, seeing double, developing a rash, feeling exhausted during the day, and just overall, feeling weird."

After several doctor visits and medical tests at the University of Alabama in Birmingham Medical Center, the doctors narrowed it down to cancer, lupus, multiple sclerosis, or a rare autoimmune disease called neurosarcoidosis. It turned out to be neurosarcoidosis, or an inflammation of my brain cells and the optic nerve. There is no known cause and no cure, but the doctor drained fluid from my brain to bring down the swelling.

It didn't seem to be life-threatening, but I developed meningitis due to the buildup of fluid on my brain, and while I was in the hospital, I began having problems with my stomach. It turned out to be quite serious. I had a ruptured appendix, and the doctor had to do emergency surgery, or I could have died, he said. I was in the hospital for 46 days. I left in a wheelchair because I had trouble walking, but after a little time on the treadmill, my strength and coordination started slowly coming back.

A little while after I got home, my friend Dr. Jerry Mosely came by the house to see how I was doing, and he became alarmed when he noticed fluid still leaking out of my head. He insisted I go back to the hospital. He is a great man and friend. I still was not settled about all that had happened to me or the length of recovery, so I went to Johns Hopkins University in Baltimore, Maryland to get a second opinion on my neurosarcoidosis diagnosis.

The female doctor there didn't tell me anything except that I was going to have to change professions.

I let her have it. "You don't know a damn thing about sports or athletics! That is not going to happen!"

My doctor at UAB put me on a steroid called Prednisone. I regained the 50 pounds I had lost, and it cleared up, but it took me a while to get back to where I could control where I hit the tennis ball. Because of my blurred vision caused by the neurosarcoidosis, I would hit it thinking I was hitting it in one direction, and it would go in another. My doctor, Gary Cowan went out to play with me after I got out of the hospital. I used to always beat him and now he was giving me a 10-point lead and still beating me every time. It took a while for me to get my coordination back caused by sarcoidosis.

The problem has recurred only once since then. I really do not know what it is, but I prayed daily, *my mind and body are great, and I will be back playing sports and competitive tennis any day*. In the past 17 years, I have had four rotator cuff surgeries, a hip replacement, gall bladder surgery, and a back operation. I had no problems recovering quickly and the hip replacement was the easiest by far.

Four years ago, I came home from work with a severe headache. Thinking a cup of coffee might help, I didn't realize the seriousness of the situation. Recognizing the signs of a stroke, I was rushed to the emergency room at Walker Baptist Medical Center and immediately airlifted to UAB. The next day, I woke up with 56 stitches in my head. I had suffered a hemorrhagic stroke with a brain bleed. Dr. Cowen consulted with the surgeon, and they agreed on a clinical trial surgery. A couple of weeks later, I told the doctor I was going home. I had enough of the hospital.

He said, "Oh no, you're not. You are a fall risk."

"Doc, I have no idea where you went to school, but I was a professional drunk for 12 years, and I am a pretty good athlete. I never fell on the ice while pin-balling around every bar in the state of Wisconsin. I'm not sitting around in this shit hole."

He refused to let me leave so I had to stay eight more days. So many friends came to see me to wish me well: Super Dave, of course, Haig Wright, Charlie Owens, Jay Todd, Dan Lucas and Shannon Johnson. Loyalty is a rare commodity, but not for these guys. I appreciate them so much. And Susan was by my side through it all, thank the Lord. Today, I am doing quite well at age 65, and still teaching tennis, but tragedy is taking some of my friends' lives and many of those from cancer like Super Dave's brother Donnie Meade.

As for the rest of my family, when my grandfather Dick passed away in his 90s, we put some of his ashes in a balloon and released it over Clear Lake at Red Pine Camp. Fifteen minutes later, a bald eagle flew alongside the balloon. I'll be honest. When my mother died of pancreatic cancer in 2014, I was devastated but I was so glad she saw me many years sober and married with a family. I realized as an adult, she was a super mom.

Robin and I did exactly the same thing with her – we put some of her ashes in a bag and tied it to a balloon and just like Dick, released it on the waterfront at Red Pine Camp on Clear Lake. Fifteen minutes later, a bald eagle flew alongside the balloon.

Everyone was in tears, and I would say it was a good grief in a way – the kind that gives me peace. ReRe also passed away in her 90s of natural causes. She was like a second mother to me. I'm grateful that both she and my mom were able to see me sober before they passed.

Stay healthy, stay positive, and enjoy your family and friends. Every day, I thank God I am still alive, still enjoy working, and look forward to watching the grandkids' journey. And above all, if you have a drinking problem, or if you suspect you may have a drinking problem, seek help. Do not hesitate. Call your local AA today!

On Politics

I thought long and hard about whether to include this section in the book. Politics is a tricky subject, and I know it can stir strong feelings on both sides. But this book is about my life, my experiences, and my perspective. And if I left this part out, I wouldn't be telling the whole story. Whether you agree with me or not, these are my honest thoughts, and if you've made it this far in the book, you know I'm not one to shy away from sharing what I believe.

People often ask me why I support Donald Trump, and it's not a question I shy away from. Politics has a way of dividing people, but my reasons aren't about party lines or trendy sound bites - they're about principles, leadership, and a willingness to fight for something bigger than yourself.

First and foremost, Trump has a kind of street smarts that you can't learn in a classroom. He built a business empire from the ground up, and you don't do that without knowing how to negotiate, how to adapt, and how to work with people from every walk of life. Building skyscrapers and managing billion-dollar deals isn't something you stumble into - it takes intelligence, resilience, and vision.

But beyond that, Trump is relatable. He doesn't act like he's better than everyone else, and he doesn't talk in circles the way most politicians do. He speaks directly and plainly, and while that sometimes rubs people the wrong way, I find it refreshing. Whether you're a billionaire in a penthouse or a guy stringing rackets at the local tennis club, Trump talks to you, not at you.

Another thing I respect about Trump is that he's a fighter. The amount of heat this man has taken - the lawsuits, the media attacks, the endless political hit jobs - would have sent most people packing. But he doesn't back down. He could have retired to the sidelines a long time ago. He doesn't need the money, and he doesn't need the spotlight. He's still in this match because he believes in America, and that kind of dedication deserves respect.

Something a lot of people might not know - and something I personally admire - is that Trump has never had a drink in his life. That's impressive on its own, but even more so when you realize the kind of circles he's run in. His brother struggled with alcoholism and told him, "Don't drink, Donald." And he never did. As someone who's walked my own road to sobriety, that kind of discipline and self-control means a lot to me.

Politically, Trump changed the landscape in ways that can't be ignored. He doesn't sugarcoat the truth or hide behind carefully scripted talking points. He speaks directly, sometimes bluntly, about issues that other politicians tiptoe around. Whether it's immigration, foreign trade, or economic policy, Trump says what he believes—and often, he's been proven right.

I know people have their criticisms, and I'm not here to tell anyone how to think. But I believe history will look back on Trump as a leader who stepped onto a court full of broken rackets and torn nets and said, "Give me the ball." I believe his legacy will be one of strength, economic recovery, and a renewed sense of pride in being American.

He reminds me of a tennis player down two sets in a five-set match, refusing to quit. When the pressure's at its highest, the best players don't double-fault - they deliver an ace. And that's exactly what Trump does.

Now, I'm not saying everyone has to agree with me, and I'm not here to change anyone's mind. I know some people see Trump differently, and that's fine. But this is how I see him.

At the end of the day, my support for Trump comes down to one word: *loyalty.* Loyalty to this country, loyalty to its people, and loyalty to the principles that built it. And as long as a leader is fighting for those things, they'll have my support.

We live in a time where it's easy to stay quiet about your beliefs, to go along with the crowd, and to avoid rocking the boat. But I've never been one to shy away from speaking my mind, and I'm not about to start now.

So, whether you agree with me or not, I hope you understand where I'm coming from. Because when it comes to the future of this country, I believe loyalty, resilience, and honesty still matter - and those are qualities I see in Donald Trump.

This book is about my story, my truth, and my perspective. Agree or disagree, I hope you'll respect that this is an important part of who I am. After all, the whole point of sharing my story is to give you an honest look at the journey I've taken - on and off the tennis court.

THOUGHTS ON ALCOHOLICS ANONYMOUS

AA is a great place for a second chance. I'll admit, when I first walked through those doors, I thought it was a place for losers. After all, I wasn't coming in with a winning hand. But over time, I learned just how much wisdom exists within those rooms.

When I first started, I was trembling with fear and anxiety, unsure if I even belonged. Yet, the people there welcomed me with open arms. "You're welcome here," they'd say. "Keep coming back." That simple phrase gave me hope when I had none. One guy shared something that stuck with me: "Just because the circus left town doesn't mean you got the monkey off your back." I later learned George Carlin, the comedian, said that, but I'm pretty sure he got it from a drunk. Only in AA could a line like that find its roots.

I thank God daily for keeping me clean and sober. I've found joy in talking with other alcoholics, sharing our struggles, and celebrating each other's victories. If you're struggling with addiction, I urge you to give AA a try. You might feel like you're beyond help or that no one understands, but you'd be surprised how much better life can get. Godspeed to anyone willing to take that first step.

AA is more than just a place to stop drinking; it's a form of counseling. It's about sharing experiences and advice with others who've walked a similar path. You leave a meeting feeling a little more uplifted, a little stronger, and often with what we call an "attitude of gratitude." There's something incredibly humbling about listening to someone who's been through hell and back, yet still stands tall.

For me, being clean and sober means clarity. My mind isn't clouded, and I no longer hear the same cruel lines I used to hear during my darkest years. From age 14 to 24, people would look at me and say, "Your eyes are like two piss holes in a snowbank." That's not a compliment, in case you're wondering. Now, those same eyes reflect something better - hope, strength, and a life reclaimed.

AA isn't about perfection; it's about progress. It's about walking into a room full of strangers and realizing you're not alone. For anyone considering this journey, know this: the road isn't easy, but it's worth every step. Keep coming back.

ACKNOWLEDGEMENTS

Looking back on the wild ride that is my life, I can't help but be filled with gratitude for the people who stuck with me through the highs and lows. They say it takes a village to raise a child, and in my case, it took a whole army to get me sober and keep me that way. This book wouldn't exist without them.

First and foremost, I want to thank my family - my mother, Sarah, who weathered more storms than any one person should, and who kept fighting to give me and my sister, Robin, a life we could be proud of. Without her strength, I wouldn't have the chance to write these words. Robin, my sister, has been there through it all. We both fought our demons, sometimes together, sometimes apart, but we never gave up. We came out stronger.

To my late father, Wayne, who I didn't get nearly enough time with, I thank you for what you gave me, even in those brief days. Your absence shaped me, but so did your presence, however fleeting.

Charles Edson, my AA sponsor, I owe you more than words can express. You called me out when I needed it and stood by me when it mattered most. Your tough love saved my life. To Tom Dugdale, my counselor, and the folks in my first AA meetings, you opened the door to a life of sobriety, and for that, I'll be forever grateful.

To Marshall, who gave me that job as a tennis instructor when I desperately needed a second chance - thank you for trusting me, despite my past, and for believing in me enough to give me a shot. You might have offered me a job at a nudist resort, but that gig helped set the stage for a lifetime of second chances.

Charlie Owens, you're one of the greatest athletes I've known, and you inspired me to be better, both on and off the court. I learned more from you than just tennis, and your friendship means the world to me.

To Super Dave and all the boys back in Minocqua - Richard, Grizz, Scott, and the rest of the gang - you made life wild, and you stood by me through the chaos. We shared some wild times, but more importantly, we shared real friendship.

Bebo, you've come a long way, and I couldn't be prouder. You were always an incredible athlete - football, basketball, tennis, you made it look effortless. Growing up with your mom, you had to be tough, and yeah, that quick temper got you into a few scrapes, but it also gave you an edge. That edge took you to a tennis scholarship at the University of North Alabama and turned you into the successful businessman you are today. You've always had that mix of raw talent, street smarts, and grit, and it's been incredible to see where it's taken you. Keep it up - you've earned every bit of your success.

Some people leave an unforgettable mark on your life, and the late Al Blanton was one of those people. He had a knack for making everyone laugh, often saying things like, "Grant, I am one hell of a poacher," and celebrating every winning point with a loud, "Tooo goood!" He'd also proudly declare, "My son, Little Al, is a genius!"

Rex Murray and Bob Maddox, two treasures of Musgrove Country Club, deserve a mention as well. Both are outstanding athletes, but their true calling is golf.

Between them, they've scored 19 holes-in-one. Every conversation with these guys is a lesson in sports and life, and I'm thankful for the wisdom and laughs they've shared with me over the years.

Of course, I can't forget about Carrie Strum, a gifted tennis pro I worked with at Bonaventure. She and her husband, Drew, a dentist, are fantastic people with a wonderful family. Now retired, Carrie plays golf daily and has become an outstanding player. It was a pleasure working with you, Carrie.

Furthermore, for anything sports-related - football, basketball, baseball, golf, tennis, auto racing, horse racing, even elections - I always call my buddy, Dr. Ricky Wade. He always has the answers, no matter the topic.

Of all the moments I've witnessed in tennis - both triumphant and heartbreaking - one stands out as the most tragic. It happened on Court 4 at Musgrove Country Club, where Dr. Charlie Bush collapsed and passed away during a match.

Charlie was more than just a familiar face on the court; he was a good man with a kind spirit and a deep love for the game. He had a wonderful family who shared in his passion for tennis, and his presence brought warmth and camaraderie to every match he played.

It's hard to put into words the weight of that day - the suddenness of it, the silence that followed, and the realization of how quickly life can change. Tennis teaches us about resilience, about fighting back after every point, but moments like that remind us of something deeper: the importance of the people we share the game with.

Charlie's legacy lives on, not just in the memories of those who knew him, but in the love for the game he passed down to others. Here's to you, Charlie.

Lastly, to my students and everyone who ever let me teach them on the tennis court - thank you for letting me be part of your journey. Coaching you has been my greatest privilege. This book is for all of you. Thanks for the lessons, the love, and the laughs.

- Grant Rolley

ABOUT THE ALBUM

As much as I love telling stories, some memories are best captured in pictures. This little collection of photos is a snapshot of my life - some from the wild days, others from the calmer ones. You'll see the faces of those who walked alongside me, the places that shaped me, and a few moments that still make me smile.

These photos aren't just for me; they're for everyone who was part of this crazy ride. From the courts to the AA meetings, from my family to my friends, these are the people and places that helped me find my way. I hope, in flipping through these images, you'll get a glimpse of the life I lived - the good, the bad, and everything in between.

Grant Rolley (right) and Shannon Johnson (left), his all-time favorite player in 1989

Grant with football Autographed by Bart Starr and Brett Favre

Grant's friends at the Hall of Fame, traveling on the bus he rented

David Meade (left) and Donnie Meade (right)

Alabama's greatest player, the legend Charlie Owens

Jeff Gray (left), Dan Lucas (right), and Grant Rolley (center) at the Alabama Hall of Fame

Boogie Franklin (left) and Grant Rolley (right)

Mike Wigginton Jr. (left), Mike Wigginton Sr. (center), and Andrew Wigginton (right)

David Meade (left) and Richard Simmons (right)

Janni Westerman (left), Oliver Wright (center), and Reed Pilling (right)

Haig Wright (left) and Grant Rolley (right), representing the number one team in the State Men's 30s age division

Grant Rolley and Dan Lucas celebrating their 8th State Title.

Jeremiah Alexander

Shannon Johnson, a standout talent and one of Walker High School's greatest players

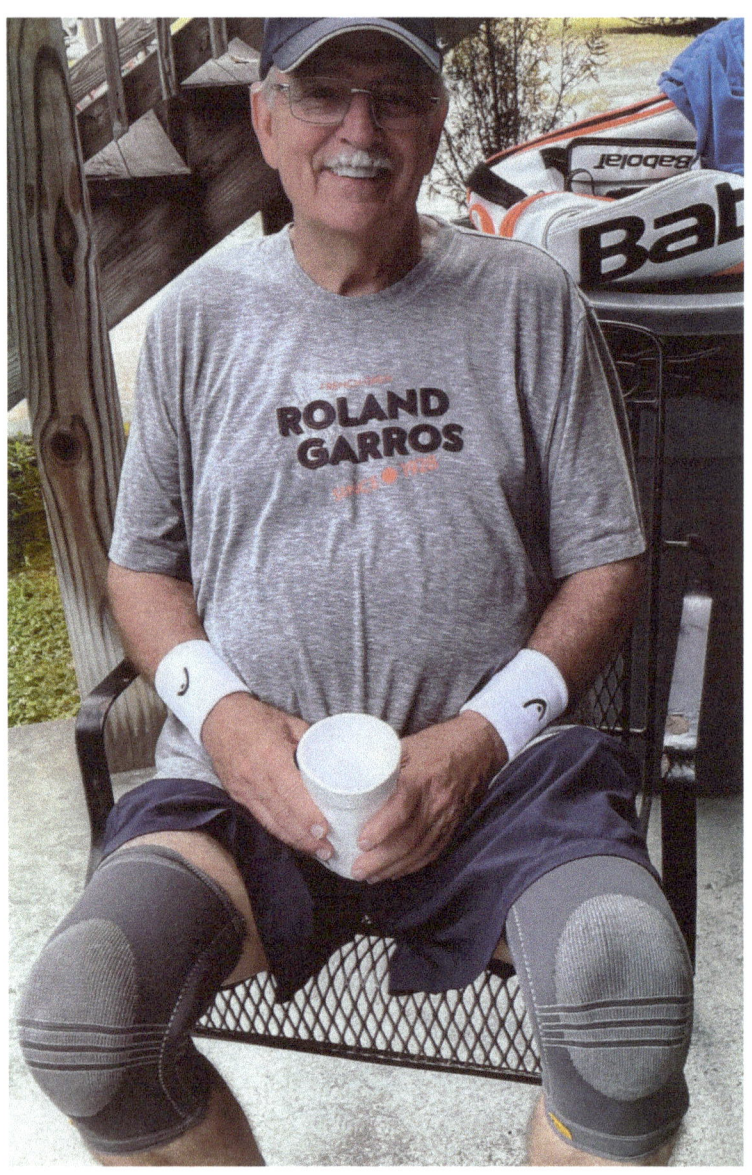

Roger "The Diamond Man" Hill

Grant Rolley (left) and Charlie Owens (right)

Grant Rolley and Coach Jay Todd with the Walker High School State Championship team

Juan Nunez (left) and Grant Rolley (right)

Bob Maddox (left) and Rex Murray (right) are both elite golf players, each boasting an impressive record of 19 hole-in-ones

Grant Rolley (bottom right) with his grandmother Helen (bottom left), mother Sarah (top left), and sister Robin (top right)

The Walker High School team celebrates another state championship victory, accompanied by Coach Jay Todd.

Mark Keil

Grant Rolley on the left and John McEnroe on the right

www.ingramcontent.com/pod-product-compliance
Lightning Source LLC
Chambersburg PA
CBHW051626120626
46551CB00014B/1953